ENDORSEMENTS

"Having worked alongside Mark Stevenson and experienced his passion and resilience, perseverance and flow firsthand, I can confidently say that Adventure Mindset is a vital resource for today's business leaders. In a world where volatility and change are constants, Mark's 22 principles provide a clear, actionable roadmap for organizations looking to evolve from merely surviving to truly thriving. This book challenges leaders to rethink their strategies, embrace uncertainty, and foster resilience within their teams. Mark's insights are not just inspiring—they are essential for any organization determined to transform chaos into opportunity and lead with confidence in an unpredictable future."

— Dr. Darren R. Weissman, Developer of
The LifeLine Technique® and Bestselling Author of
The Power of Infinite Love & Gratitude

Choose adventure—Choose this book! Mark Stevenson brings a unique blend of insight, wisdom, and adventure that makes the hairs stand up on the back of your neck! Highly recommended!

— Kirsty Maynor, CEO, The Firefly Group.
Bestselling Author of Untangled: A Guide to Change
You Choose and Change You Don't

This is a guide to becoming the kind of person the world needs right now. Each principle offers a meaningful invitation to deepen self-awareness, stretch beyond comfort, and step into life with greater courage, purpose, and resilience.

— Ken Honda, Bestselling Author of "Happy Money: The Japanese Art of Making Peace With Your Money" and numerous other titles in Japan (where he is well-known for writing books on money and happiness, with book sales surpassing eight million copies since 2001)

Mark Stevenson has written a masterpiece. With the spirit of an explorer and the clarity of a seasoned guide, he takes us on a journey that is both deeply personal and profoundly practical. Adventure Mindset doesn't just present ideas, it invites introspection, advocates for courage, and equips us with tools to thrive in a volatile world. Each principle pulses with authenticity and lived experience. The interweaving of wisdom traditions, scientific perspectives, peppered with vivid storytelling, is simply superb. If you're serious about becoming the best version of yourself, in work, leadership, or life, this book is a must-read. I'll be recommending it to every intentional leader I know.

— Lewis Senior, CEO Equilibria, Podcast Host of the Intentional CEO, and International Bestselling author of Personalities Remixed

Adventure Mindset by Mark Stevenson is a compelling guide to rethinking how we approach uncertainty, challenge, and growth. With clarity and optimism, Stevenson explores how cultivating curiosity and courage can transform both personal and professional landscapes. A must-read for anyone navigating change or seeking to lead with resilience, purpose and intentionality.

— Paul Grant, Co-founder of Equilibria and
International Bestselling author of Money Remixed
and Personalities Remixed

What struck me most about Adventure Mindset is its relevance—not just for leaders or entrepreneurs, but for anyone navigating change. Mark's voice is clear, wise, and grounded. This book doesn't just inform—it transforms.

— Judy O'Beirn, President of
Hasmark Publishing International

"One great way to build an Adventure Mindset is to randomly read a single chapter from the book. You'll find its wisdom feeding you throughout the days to come. This will deliver to you the Adventure Mindset in bite-sized and practical pieces that are interesting, profound, engaging, and compounding."

— Pete Bissonette, President,
Learning Strategies

ADVENTURE MINDSET

22 Principles for Growing & Thriving Amidst Chaos & Change

By
Mark L. Stevenson

Plumb Road Publishing
Palo Alto

Published by
Plumb Road Publishing
Palo Alto
www.plumbroadpublishing.com

Copyright © 2025 Mark Stevenson
First Edition

All Rights Reserved.

No part of this book may be reproduced or transmitted in any form or by any means, electronic or mechanical, including photocopying, recording or by any information storage and retrieval system, without written permission from the author, except for the inclusion of brief quotations in a review.

Disclaimer

This book is designed to provide information and motivation to our readers. It is sold with the understanding that the neither the publisher nor the author is engaged to render any type of psychological, legal, or any other kind of professional advice. No warranties or guarantees are expressed or implied by any of the content in this volume. Neither the publisher nor the author shall be liable for any physical, psychological, emotional, financial, or commercial damages, including, but not limited to, special, incidental, consequential or other damages. Our views and rights are the same: You are responsible for your own choices, actions, and results.

Permission requests should be addressed in writing to info@PlumbRoadPublishing.com

Library of Congress Control Number: 2025915338

Editor: Cate Montana cate@catemontana.com
Cover Design: Anne Karklins anne@hasmarkpublishing.com
Interior Layout: Amit Dey amit@hasmarkpublishing.com

ISBN 13: 978-0-9799252-5-2
ISBN 10: : 0-9799252-5-2

DEDICATION

This book is dedicated to my parents and grandparents and all those who came before me and along with me who helped me look for ways to have compassion for others and take action to be helpful in some way.

and

This book is dedicated to all those coming forth who imagine and see life as an adventure to relish and learn from, no matter how big or small.

You are my inspiration.

PREFACE

The only way to make sense out of change is to plunge into it, move with it, and join the dance.

~ Alan Watts

Adventure means different things to different people. I've had some extraordinary adventures out in the wilds of nature, and some in the work world as well.

In 2008 I had a front row seat in the financial markets as the great financial crisis unfolded, and I came to see it as an adventure. Surely that would be the biggest adventure of this ilk in my lifetime. Then, in early March 2023 I was with Silicon Valley Bank when the extreme chaos of a bank run unfolded at astonishing speed.

I was in an all-day meeting where we were planning for the rest of the year. We weren't too deep into the morning's agenda when everyone's phone started ringing and pinging and buzzing. Clients were wanting to know why things weren't working - why the important wires they scheduled had not been activated; or why certain transactions were delayed. And why is the stock price in freefall? We adjourned the meeting to turn our attention to what was unfolding. None of us imagined what would happen over the coming days.

I thought I'd seen nearly everything over the years, but this was an extreme level of pandemonium new to all of us. Tens of billions of dollars were wired out of the bank in a matter of hours, with more wire requests in the queue. SVB's relatively few traditional branches were overwhelmed as clients showed up in person, lining up at the front doors, fearing that their money could evaporate. Additional chaos played out in the electronic systems, as many others acted via their online portal and mobile devices.

Everyone was trying to accomplish the same thing at the same time—move as much money as possible out of the bank. It was a massive, desperate, frenzy. Entire companies and great fortunes were at risk. Critical transactions were in process, involving many millions of dollars that now couldn't happen. Some companies were in the midst of processing payroll to pay their employees, and other longtime clients couldn't get access to their funds when they needed them.

All this weighed heavily on my mind as I had many conversations with clients at all hours of the day and night. As the systems froze, the ability for my colleagues and me to help them was stifled. Then, everything stopped. SVB had been seized by the FDIC.

The flow of money between companies and people in the economy is as vital as oxygen. Everything stops without it, and deprived for too long, people (and companies) cannot function and may cease to exist.

The FDIC did what it was there to do - stave off a broader panic that might have rippled to all corners of the economy, then determine the fate of the entity. Eventually movement of funds was restored, and the panic and chaos subsided, though uncertainty remained the constant. Much is still to be written about the causes of these chaotic events of March 2023 and where blame should be assigned. While those events were a catalyst for me to write this book, my intent here is to focus on how we best equip ourselves for dealing with chaos when it does arise. And it appears that the frequency and intensity of chaos and change is accelerating. So, no time like the present.

Adventuring has always attracted me. I could test my limits, stretch my thinking, summon my courage. There is much that I've learned while adventuring which can be applied to the rest of life, including how we choose to show up in times of uncertainty, change, and chaos. Real adventures can contain moments and situations we'd rather not be dealing with. Not everything is solvable, however by enhancing our skills we can make choices that lead to action to increase the probability of our success.

The writing process for this book led me to identify principles of successful adventuring that might be applicable more broadly. I narrowed the initial list (of over 35) down to 22 principles; a number that felt right in the 'middle path.' Some may find this too many or too few, but it represents my attempt at comprehensive yet practical guidance. You will see wisdom, old and new, in this collection. Successful exploration often requires surviving and thriving in extreme conditions, and much ancient wisdom applies to this. The principles address both individual development and group dynamics, as adventures can be solo or collaborative endeavors.

Whatever stage you are in life, you will find principles here that can make a difference in how you experience life.

Whether you are part of formal organizations—teams, non-profit NGOs, educational institutions, government entities, traditional companies or startups—or have no formal affiliations, see yourself as a free agent, or world vagabond, these principles are designed to apply broadly to human interactions and challenges.

These principles draw from ancient wisdom spanning warfare to peaceful cultural exchanges that are applicable across diverse settings and circumstances. For grammatical efficiency, I may reference 'business,' 'company,' or 'enterprise' when discussing organizational functions, but my intention is broader application.

A note about "*Adventure Mindset*": I view '*mind*' as encompassing one's full body and being, including heart and spirit—not just brain activity. Like Shunryu Suzuki's "Zen Mind, Beginner's Mind," this represents a 'full-beingness' approach to life, though English lacks sufficient words to capture this concept fully and succinctly. The '*set*' portion might suggest something fixed, but this isn't about establishing rigid frameworks. Adventure is dynamic and requires an equally dynamic mindset. As you'll see, dealing with accelerating change and chaos requires continuously evolving approaches.

Thank you for picking up this book to explore the realm of adventure wisdom. That means you have curiosity and a penchant for looking beyond the ordinary. At this moment in human history, we need more people willing to embrace uncertainty, find opportunity in challenge, and approach life with the mind, heart, and spirit of an adventurer…because life itself is the greatest adventure of all.

Thank you for embracing the adventure and joining the dance!

TABLE OF CONTENTS

Preface ix

Introduction 1

Principle #1: Acceptance of Impermanence, Change, and Interconnectedness 11

Principle #2: Awareness of Self, Situation, and Others .. 23

Principle #3: Authenticity: Know Thy Self, Be Thy Self 35

Principle #4: Reside in Choice 43

Principle #5: Values: Their Role in Decision-Making & Organizational Success 53

Principle #6: Communal Self-reliance: The Power of Collaborative Interdependence 65

Principle #7: Empathy and Compassion: The Cornerstone of Human Connection 77

Principle #8: Cultivate Presence 83

Principle #9: Equanimity: Stillness Within 93

Principle #10: Prepared Spontaneity 103

Principle #11: Inspiration and Vision 1.0 113

Principle #12: Purpose and Meaningful Service 125

Principle #13: Responsibility and Accountability: The Foundation of Human Potential ... 131

Principle #14: Strategic Patience ... 141

Principle #15: Gratitude and the Alchemy of Appreciation and Wonder ... 151

Principle #16: Reciprocity and Generosity: The Foundations for Thriving ... 159

Principle #17: Stewardship: Caring for What Supports and Sustains ... 169

Principle #18: Seek Wisdom: Discernment, Curiosity, Continuous Learning, & Critical Thinking ... 181

Principle #19: Mindful Creativity, Innovation, and *"Something Else"* ... 191

Principle #20: Confident Humility and Inner Security . 199

Principle #21: Vision 2.0: The Vision Quest of the Spirit . 215

Principle #22: Transcendence and Transformation 225

Concluding Thoughts: Making Adventure Principles Work for You ... 243

Acknowledgements ... 249

About the Author ... 253

Notes ... 255

Index ... 263

INTRODUCTION

All great changes are preceded by chaos

~ Deepak Chopra

Standing on a remote overlook of the Karnali River in western Nepal with a friend and co-member of our nine-person kayak river-running expedition, we were assessing the scene awaiting us as we embarked on the next leg of our journey. We knew this was likely to be a particularly gnarly part of the river, we just didn't know the extent. Breaking the silence, I hear these words: *"You know you're on an adventure when in that moment you wish you were back home talking about it instead…"*

The parallels between wilderness exploration and navigating today's world are striking. Just as explorers face unpredictable weather, uncertain terrain, and constant challenges, people of all types; entrepreneurs, educators, and leaders of organizations of all sizes, now navigate rapidly shifting markets, evolving technologies, and unprecedented global challenges. The skills that enabled explorers to thrive—adaptability, resilience, comfort with uncertainty—are precisely what we need today, both in the business world and in our personal lives.

In a world where change is the only constant, the adventure perspective and mindset isn't just helpful—it's essential for survival and success. Just as traditional explorers required specific skills to thrive in uncharted territories, we now need the adventure mindset and the skills that go with it to navigate and thrive in our rapidly evolving world.

As a young person I read the book *Future Shock* by Alvin Toffler. The title was apropos for the times as a warning about humanity's increasing difficulty in coping with accelerating change. Today, his predictions seem almost quaint compared to the reality we face. The pace of change in our world has moved beyond linear progression to exponential acceleration, creating what scientists call a VUCA environment—Volatile, Uncertain, Complex, and Ambiguous.[1]

The typical smartphone in most peoples' pockets has more computing power than all of the combined NASA Apollo missions that put the first humans on the moon. Technologies that seemed like science fiction a decade ago—artificial intelligence, genetic engineering, quantum computing—are daily reshaping our world. This acceleration isn't limited to technology, it permeates every aspect of our lives, from climate patterns to social structures, from economic systems to workplace dynamics.

Traditional approaches to success built on assumptions of stability and predictability are crumbling in this new reality. The five-year plan, once a cornerstone of strategy, now is obsolete before it's implemented. The career ladder has transformed into something more resembling a rock-climbing wall, requiring constant adaptation and multiple paths to progress. Which brings me to the adventure mindset.

Researchers are finding that conventional success strategies fall short in today's environment of accelerating change because organizations and individuals that rely on traditional, stability-based approaches experience less success than those who are able to innovate and navigate major changes effectively—abilities which are a natural part of the adventure mindset.

The psychological benefits of viewing challenges as adventures are particularly relevant in our high-stress era. When we approach change and uncertainty with an adventure orientation, we can experience what psychologists call "eustress," the positive form of stress that energizes and motivates us. This perspective activates our brain's capacity for rewiring and growth, improving problem-solving abilities and emotional resilience. An adventure mindset also stimulates personal growth while facilitating an open mind and relaxation around uncertainty.[2]

Individuals who adopt an adventure perspective show significantly higher levels of innovation, job satisfaction, and mental well-being. They're also more likely to identify opportunities in chaos and create successful solutions to complex problems.

The adventure mindset

When we examine what makes something an adventure, four core elements emerge: 1) uncertainty, 2) newness or novelty, 3) challenge, and 4) the potential for growth. These elements are present not only in traditional adventures like mountain climbing or ocean exploration, but also in the pivotal moments of our personal and professional lives. In its truest sense, adventure extends far beyond the realm of physical expeditions. It's a mindset, a way of approaching life's challenges and uncertainties that transforms obstacles into opportunities for growth while transforming people into lifelong pioneers along the way.

When Erik Weihenmayer reached the summit of Mount Everest in 2001, he became the first blind person to achieve this feat. But what perhaps is more remarkable is how he translated the mindset of courage, indomitability, and perseverance that got him to that summit into transformative success in other areas of life. Erik went on to found No Barriers USA, an organization that has helped thousands of people with disabilities break through their own limitations. His story, and others in the book, exemplify a profound truth: The principles that drive success in adventure can catalyze extraordinary achievements in any domain.

Throughout my life, I have sought adventure. In my early years it came in the form of mountain climbing, kayaking wild-water rivers, hopping freight trains, and solo hiking remote regions of the world—most of which carried intense dangers and made extreme physical and psychological demands. Frankly, I was lucky to survive some of those adventures, many of which required making fast, accurate situational assessments, often in life and death situations. But the time spent pursuing these physical challenges trained me to accept personal responsibility and develop a mental and emotional flexibility and

> *"You know you're on an adventure when there are moments that you wish you are back home talking about it instead."*

resilience that has enabled me to face risk and succeed in other endeavors in my life, both personal and professional. Any meaningful adventure involves risk, uncertainty, and the possibility of disappointment. Even, in some cases, the threat of accident and death. But developing the skills of the adventure mindset mitigates the danger. And the adventures themselves—whether in the wilds of nature or the wilds of commerce—ultimately offer the potential for extraordinary rewards. Which is why I decided to take the risk and write this book. The adventure mindset is a valuable asset no matter what you're doing.

I've known founders of companies, technology professionals, VCs, scientists, and people in many other fields of expertise who made courageous decisions in their lives and careers and pursued what sometimes seemed to be impossible dreams. The journeys these people took contained the same elements that define traditional adventures: the uncertainty of venturing into unknown territory, the challenge of building something new, and the tremendous potential for both personal growth and positive impact on the world. By approaching their journeys with an adventure perspective, they transformed what could have been overwhelming uncertainties into doable challenges (with no guarantees), and exciting quests for innovation.

Business and leadership applications

The transferable skills from adventure to everyday life are numerous and profound. For example, American rock climber and environmentalist Yvon Chouinard took his expedition skills and environmental ethics into the business world, founding the company Patagonia, a billion-dollar recreational retail brand that revolutionized corporate responsibility practices with its commitment to product excellence and environmental sustainability.

Or let's take risk assessment. When American high-altitude mountaineer Ed Viesturs evaluates whether to continue his ascent on a 21,000-foot Himalayan peak in a blizzard or turn back, he employs the same decision-making framework that successful business leaders use when evaluating market opportunities. Both scenarios require careful analysis of potential rewards against risks, consideration of available resources, and the wisdom to know when to persist versus when to pivot.

Core transferable skills include:

- Strategic resource management
- Adaptive leadership under pressure
- Resilience in the face of setbacks
- Dynamic problem-solving
- Team coordination in challenging conditions
- Clear communication during uncertainty
- Integrating lessons from every event
- Capacity to pivot at any moment

In essence, we're discussing "calculated audacity." The kind of informed boldness that American rock climber Alex Honnold exhibited when, after years of preparation, he conducted his famous 2017 free solo climb of El Capitan in Yosemite National Park—a climb that *The New York Times* described as "One of the great athletic feats of any kind, ever."

Introduction

And yet this kind of "calculated audacity" is exactly what companies in the innovation economy have long engaged, taking enormous but carefully calculated risks to push the boundaries of what's possible. This isn't reckless chance-taking, but rather strategic risk management informed by thorough preparation and clear purpose. In other words, projects fully engaging the adventure mindset.

Your adventure profile

Self-knowledge is a basic requirement for adventure. Before any significant adventure begins, whether it's scaling a mountain, transforming an organization, or learning the principles outlined in this book, proper preparation is essential. So, let's start with understanding your adventure profile and your current relationship with change and uncertainty. Consider the following questions:

- When faced with unexpected challenges, what's your typical first response?
- How do you feel when plans change suddenly?
- What's the biggest risk you've taken in the last year, and how did you handle it? What's the biggest risk you've taken in your life? How did it turn out? How has this affected you're subsequent thinking?
- In what situations do you feel most alive and engaged?
- What's your adventure threshold? (The point where excitement meets fear, where challenge meets capability)

Your adventure threshold isn't fixed. Where you start isn't where you end up. It's more like a muscle that can be strengthened over time. Swiss adventurer and explorer Sarah Marquis didn't just launch herself into her 20,000-kilometer solo walk from Siberia to the Gobi Desert, into China, Laos, and Thailand. She began with short solo hikes getting herself into a state of ever-greater "adventure fitness" (not just physical readiness) before she headed out on her three-year sojourn in 2010.

And "adventure fitness" – body-mind-spirit – is exactly what this book is designed to help bring you.

A few quick tips

The principles explained in this book can be learned and applied by anyone. But the way they're experienced and embodied will vary. Introverts reading this might lean more toward internal exploration and reflection, while extroverts might decide to dive straight into external applications at work or in personal relationships. Whatever your personality type, reflecting upon and adapting the principles presented here in ways that suit your natural strengths will help this journey stay authentic and enlivening.

Every principle ends with a set of questions to reflect on. I highly recommend not skipping them to rush on to the next principle. "Rushing" and "adventure" are not wise bedfellows. The whole point of the book is to help you understand, embody, and then apply the adventure mindset—to make it your own and find success from the learning. And the questions at the end of each principle are designed to help you do just that. Take them seriously. When you do, you'll

> "Rushing" and "adventure" are not wise bedfellows.

already be applying Principle 2: Awareness, and Principle 14: Strategic Patience.

Finally, as you learn the adventure mindset, it will be instructive to pay attention to how successful individuals and organizations are implementing these ideas. How are company leaders navigating disruptive markets? How are educators fostering student resilience? How are community organizers building social change movements? Who in your circle is the one always seeing the possibility of an exciting journey ahead? Where do you see the adventure mindset in play? Where is it absent?

By examining individuals and organizations that have embraced adventure thinking and watching those who are *not* implementing it, you will gain insights into how to bring these principles to life in your own experience, transforming challenges into opportunities and creating sustainable success for yourself in this rapidly evolving world.

So, now ... onward!

PRINCIPLE #1

ACCEPTANCE OF IMPERMANENCE, CHANGE, AND INTERCONNECTEDNESS

Change is the only constant in life.

~ Heraclitus

Traditional success strategies are increasingly inadequate in the face of accelerating change. However, embracing an adventure mindset perspective offers significant psychological benefits, including positive forms of stress that energize, motivate, and enhance problem-solving abilities and emotional resilience. This perspective fosters higher levels of innovation and mental well-being, all crucial for navigating modern challenges and achieving long-term success. While adventure is classically defined by four core elements—uncertainty, newness, challenge, and the potential for growth—my friend on the Karnali River in Nepal offered a more instinctive definition: *"You know you're on an adventure when there are moments you wish you are back home talking about it instead"*. This more practical definition underscores that true adventures inherently involve intense challenge, risk, and even a desire to escape a present difficulty; yet, it is precisely through navigating these uncomfortable moments that transformative growth occurs.

Rapidly changing weather conditions transform a calm day into a raging storm within minutes; a sudden rockslide changes a climbing route that's been planned for months; unexpected equipment failures, lost food rations, falls, injuries, entrapment, political coup d'etats and sudden military action in unexpected places... any expedition is subject to unforeseen change. Years of planning and arduous training can go up in smoke in a heartbeat.

Few adventurers know this better than long-distance swimmer Diana Nyad who started swimming competitively at the age of ten. At age 29 she swam 102 miles from the Bahamas to Juno Beach, Florida, the longest ocean swim in history at that point. Her first attempt at swimming from Cuba to Florida in 1978 had to be abandoned because of unexpectedly rough seas. In 2011, at age 62, she tried it again—three times—and failed. Two attempts had to be aborted because of an asthma attack and jellyfish stings. A fourth attempt failed because a lightning storm unexpectedly changed course, endangering her life. Finally, in September 2012 at age 64, after four failed attempts across a span of 32 years, after 60 hours in the water, she crawled ashore on Smathers Beach, having swum 110.86 miles nonstop from Havana to Key West.

From my own experiences mountaineering, river running, sailing, and exploring, I can verify that dramatic shifts in conditions—be it weather, resources, or frightening encounters with bears or guerilla soldiers with automatic rifles— serve as a powerful reminder of the fundamental nature of our reality: Everything is in constant flux, everything is impermanent, everything is interconnected, and the only thing we can do is be as prepared as possible and then deal with whatever shows up as best we can.

> **Nothing endures unchanged for even a moment, from our thoughts and emotions to the cells in our bodies and the mountains that appear eternal.**

The shifting ways of nature

The concept of life's impermanence is hardly new. According to the Buddhist teaching of "Anicca," one of the most sophisticated philosophical treatments on change that I know, everything in existence is in a constant state of flux. Nothing endures unchanged for even a moment, from our thoughts and emotions to the cells in our bodies and the mountains that appear eternal.

John P. Milton, author, meditation and qigong master, environmentalist, and founder of the conscious global movement Way of Nature, has essentialized this ancient Eastern understanding and other spiritual traditions in twelve principles representing core principles of earth-honoring traditional lineages. Unsurprisingly, the first principle is "All Forms Are Interconnected, Constantly Change and Continuously Arise from and Return to Primordial Source". Here is John's first principle in its entirety:

> "All material forms and all energetic, perceptual, sensate, emotional and thought forms are totally interconnected and interdependent. Also, all these forms, including the sense of individual self, are

constantly changing and transforming. Fundamentally, all forms are in a continuous process of arising from, manifesting within and dissolving back into Primordial, essentially Formless, Source Awareness. At a deep level, all forms are transient and empty of permanent being. At the deepest level all forms, including ourselves, are a magical display of the Boundless, Formless Source that is our true Essence. We have the choice of either resisting this fundamental truth, and suffering; or surrendering into this truth - and dancing in the Flow."[3]

A long-time friend and spiritual teacher, John teaches that we have a choice of either resisting this fundamental truth and suffering or surrendering into this truth and dancing in the inevitable flow of life that brings new opportunities even as old dependable structures crumble.

Interconnectedness

Observing nature, we can see how no element in an ecosystem exists in isolation. Indigenous traditions have always known this, emphasizing the interconnected web of life and the importance of maintaining harmony within it. During travels in Australia, I learned of the Australian Aboriginal concept of "Dreamtime" or "The Dreaming," which reveals a complex understanding of the interconnected nature of all things across time and space. In the aboriginal view, a "nation" is a living entity that includes all things—land, water, air, animals, plants, people, stories, and songs—representing a sophisticated systems thinking that modern ecology is only now beginning to fully appreciate.

A perspective that Kenyan environmentalist and Nobel Peace Prize winner Wangari Maathai points to is that in the traditional African view, there is no separation between human beings and their environment, between the sacred and the secular, between nature and nurture. This more modern observation is in complete agreement with the famous words of Chief Sealth of the Suquamish and Duwamish peoples of the Pacific Northwest who said way back in the 1850s: "Humankind has not woven the web of life. We are but one thread within it. Whatever we do to the web, we do to ourselves. All things are bound together. All things connect."[4]

The science of interconnection

This indigenous wisdom aligns with the views of scientists like Albert Einstein and others. When Einstein said "The greatest illusion in this world is the illusion of separation," he wasn't speaking metaphorically. He was addressing the profound truth that at the subatomic level, all "things" are actually energy and thus not "things" at all. He recognized that the apparent boundaries between objects and between ourselves and our environment were illusionary as well. Instead of boundaries separating stars, planets, cows, people, bicycles, and trees, the cosmos is made up of ever-shifting, interpenetrating fields of energy.

Key scientific discoveries that demonstrate this interconnectedness include the phenomenon of quantum entanglement. Particles, for example electrons, that have bumped into each other once, remain intimately connected regardless of the distance separating them. If the "spin state" of one of these electrons changes, the spin state of the electron it bumped into a million years ago instantaneously changes as well—even across thousands of light years of space. This is not about information traveling faster than light, which would violate Einstein's theory of relativity. Instead, it suggests a deeper, non-local connection between the particles, a connection that transcends our classical understanding of space and time.

Another fascinating aspect of quantum interconnectedness is found in the concept of holography. A hologram stores information about an entire three-dimensional image across its entire two-dimensional surface. Every pixel on a hologram contains information *about the entire scene*. This principle has been extended to the universe itself, suggesting that every point in space contains information about the entire universe, just as every point on a hologram contains information about the entire image.

These scientific findings challenge our classical understanding of reality and suggest that the universe is far more interconnected than we perceive. The implications are profound, hinting at a convergence that offers a powerful foundation for addressing contemporary challenges from environmental conservation to social justice through a more holistic and interconnected lens.

Modern relevance

The recent COVID pandemic provides a stark reminder of our global interconnectedness. A virus emerging in one place rapidly spread worldwide, affecting not just health systems but also supply chains, economies, and social structures.

Acceptance of Impermanence, Change, and Interconnectedness

This clearly demonstrates how our modern world functions as a complex, interconnected system where local changes can have global repercussions.

Similarly, global supply chains highlight our deep interdependence. A semiconductor shortage in Asia can halt automobile production in Europe, while a blocked canal in the Mediterranean can affect retail prices in China. These connections aren't just economic, they're also cultural, technological, and environmental.

The work of meteorologist Edward Lorenz shows how small changes to a complex system's developing conditions can produce dramatically different outcomes. Known as the "Butterfly Effect," his calculations show that effects as small as the flap of a butterfly's wings in one part of the world can make a tiny change to the conditions of the atmosphere that eventually contribute to the formation of a tornado somewhere else on the planet.[5] Applying this phenomenon to the workings of any organization or even in a family or group of friends, consider how a small change made in one area can have an unintended effect on part or all of the whole. No matter how siloed the system or organization, it's all interconnected. And, to a large degree because of this, the pace of change is rapidly accelerating, particularly in technological and social domains. Consider that:

- The time between major technological innovations is shrinking and adoption of the newest technologies is happening at lightning speed
- Social movements can now emerge and spread globally within days

- The lifespan of companies has decreased dramatically
- Climate change is accelerating natural systems changes
- The effect of political policies reach far beyond their origin source—to the betterment or detriment of the lives of millions.

Given the magnitude and acceleration of change humanity is facing, we must be prepared to re-think <u>everything</u>. Change may arrive in the form of scenarios beyond even our wildest imagination. Just look at the impact the adoption of Artificial Intelligence has had in a few short years! We need ideas and practices to keep us grounded and present while navigating turbulent times. We need to uplevel our creative thinking as we anticipate, adapt to, or leapfrog potential changes—both personal and global. And adopting the adventure mindset and embracing the principles supporting it can help you step into the unknown with curiosity and a profound sense of preparation.

We may not know where this adventure is taking us, but with these twenty-two principles we have tools to help us on the journey.

Practical benefits

Here are just a few of the practical benefits of embracing the reality of impermanence and interconnectedness:

For Individuals:
- **Discernment in decision making**: Understanding interconnections helps us anticipate indirect consequences of our actions.

- **Move from anxiety to self-confidence**: Accepting change as natural rather than threatening is a pre-cursor to lowering stress and fear about the future. A self-confidence arises knowing that you have tools to optimize your experience.
- **Increased resilience**: Recognizing impermanence helps us bounce back from setbacks, trusting that they, too, shall pass.
- **Enhanced relationships**: Acknowledging our interconnectedness fosters empathy and cooperation.

For Businesses and Organizations:

- **Adaptive planning**: Develop flexible frameworks that can adapt to (or dare I say dance in the flow of) changing circumstances.
- **Expanded risk management**: Understanding systemic connections illuminates potential risks and opportunities.
- **Systems thinking**: Train teams to see the bigger picture and consider the broader systemic implications of decisions rather than focusing solely on immediate outcomes.
- **Smarter change navigation**: Organizations that accept change as normal are prepared to adapt more smoothly to new circumstances.
- **Resilient design**: Build systems and processes that are "anti-fragile" and prepared

- to accommodate unexpected or unplanned change rather than trying to prevent it.

- **Amplified innovation**: Embracing the fact that change is the constant creates a culture more conducive to potential breakthrough innovation.

- **Collaborative approaches**: Foster cooperation across traditional boundaries, recognizing that complex challenges require integrated solutions—dropping territorialism and self-interest in favor of relationship building and shared benefit.

- **Creating sustainable practices**: Recognizing interconnections can lead to more holistic, sustainable decision-making that considers the impact of the organization's choices, both positive or negative, for years and even generations to come.

Conclusion

Whether we're swimming oceans, running organizations, or pursuing personal goals, the acceptance of impermanence, change, and interconnectedness is a practical approach to navigating an increasingly complex and rapidly changing world. The challenge isn't to somehow stop change or manage all connections. That's impossible. Instead, the opportunity lies in learning to flow with change while being mindful of the ripple effects of our actions. As we face increasing global challenges, from climate change to technological disruption, this understanding becomes not just helpful but essential for our collective survival and flourishing.

As astronaut Jessica Meir shared in a tweet from the International Space Station in March of 2020 as the COVID pandemic was making its way around the globe: *"From up here, it is easy to see that we are truly all in this together."*

Reflective questions

As you contemplate these questions and the questions at the end of other principles, consider journaling your responses and various ideas that come to mind in order to better apply those insights in practical ways to your personal and professional life.

1. Consider a team, organization, community, or entity that you are part of. What "ripple effects" have you observed where one change led to unexpected consequences elsewhere in the system? What did this teach you about organizational interconnectedness?

2. Looking ahead the next three years, what changes do you anticipate in your field or industry? How might embracing impermanence help you or your organization prepare for and adapt to these changes more effectively?

3. Think about a significant decision you need to make. How would deeply understanding the interconnected ripple effects of this decision change your approach? What additional factors would you consider?

4. In your role as a leader or team member, how might acknowledging your fundamental interconnectedness change the way you approach collaboration and decision-making? What would you do differently?
5. Considering our accelerating rate of global change, what specific skills or capacities do you feel called to develop to help create more sustainable solutions for collective flourishing?

Tip:

As you reflect on the questions throughout this book, try to stay open and curious. Be courageously honest with yourself, yet not judgmental. This is about knowing yourself better. It's an exercise in growth, not an exam! Just sit with any discomfort that might arise and let it teach you what you need to know.

Remember, in any opportunity for growth, the goal is not perfection, but betterment.

PRINCIPLE #2

AWARENESS OF SELF, SITUATION, AND OTHERS

*It's not what you look at that matters,
it's what you see.*

~ Henry David Thoreau

Many years ago, in one of my first photography classes, the professor asked us what the difference was between "looking" and "seeing." I've pondered that question frequently over the years, and the best answer I've come up with is "seeing involves awareness." Look at a tree or a warehouse, and you get a tree or a warehouse. But "seeing" the tree or the warehouse you become aware of nuance. Variations in textures and colors. Light and shadow. Relationships. Boundaries. Space. Movement. You become aware of aesthetics or the lack thereof. Age and the passage of time. You become aware of the story of the tree and the warehouse. And stories contain meaning.

Since that photography class, I've learned how important

The greatest journey is not across terrain, but within ourselves.

awareness is for navigating life. How much it adds. For example, sitting still in wilderness places in an open-eyed meditation, taking in all the details from the subtle shift of wind through tall grasses and trees, the movement of birds and other animals in the layered textures of rock and sky, I've learned life lessons. Like how generous nature is—how free the air is, how much support the earth gives, how all lifeforms work together in harmony ... (lessons all of humanity would do well to learn.) And this kind of awareness changed me.

I remember doing a 28-day wilderness solo retreat in the mountains of central Colorado. After taking a few days to scout locations in the mountains above Crestone, I decided on a beautiful spot on a ridgeline at about 11,000 ft (3,350 m) elevation, away from the main trail where I would not likely encounter other people.

Before setting up my small tent on the first evening of that long adventure, I spent time taking a closer look around the area before darkness set in. There was a faint trail used by animals nearby, and as I followed it along the ridgeline, I reached a spot about a hundred paces up the ridge from where I planned to set up my tent. There I found what was unmistakable evidence of a mountain lion nearby—a very large pile of fresh scat.

Now, if you have experience with cats—even domestic cats—you'll know that they will sometimes use excrement to mark their territory to make the statement "I live here." It was all too easy to imagine a large cat—an apex predator weighing close to 200 pounds (~ 100 kilos)—choosing that spot to make its presence known. It was likely not far away. So, I studied the landscape carefully to see if I could locate it in the fading light of dusk. I didn't see a mountain lion, but it may well have been in a place where it could see me.

With no real weapon, not even much of a knife to defend myself, if that mountain lion wanted to eat me for dinner that night ... or the next or the next, it was certainly large enough to take me on as prey. I was aware of that. But I was also aware of how predators operate. They respect each other. And humans are predators just as much as mountain lions.

I was aware that I was encroaching on its territory. That I was a guest in its home. And so, I did my best to show reverence and respect for that large cat and its beautiful home in those amazing mountains. As well, being aware of the reciprocal nature of nature, I deliberately "put out"—or emanated—the energy of respect and lack of threat. And I envisioned equal respect and lack of threat in return. Which meant instead of spending that night and all the rest of my nights on that mountain worrying about being eaten, I just surrendered to whatever was next. Which resulted in 28 magnificent days of solo time spent meditating, practicing qigong and tai chi, communing with nature. I am confident that mountain lion saw me, and there were times I had a sense it might be nearby, but the boundary of mutual respect and awareness held. I continued to see fresh scat, but I never did see that mountain lion during those four weeks there.

Layers of awareness

Deep awareness is not a passive state. It is an active, dynamic engagement with the world—a sophisticated dance between inner perception and external reality that all indigenous cultures are aware of and have practiced for survival. Think

> **Deep awareness is a living compass, constantly recalibrating, always pointing toward deeper understanding.**

of awareness as a living compass, constantly recalibrating, always pointing toward deeper understanding.

For modern mountaineers like Reinhold Messner, awareness became the difference between life and death. During the Italian explorer's groundbreaking solo ascent of Mt. Everest, Messner didn't just look at the 29,031' mountain, he saw and *read* it. He learned to accurately interpret the language of every ice formation, wind pattern, and subtle atmospheric change—a skill he depended upon even more for survival when, along with Austrian mountaineer Peter Habeler, he climbed Everest again—this time *without supplemental oxygen*.[6]

But the benefits of awareness extend far beyond extreme environments. In other areas of life, such as in relationships, in personal growth, awareness is the difference between reacting and responding, between getting lost and finding your way.

Awareness also has layers to it. Imagine it as a multi-layered terrain that includes:

1. **Self-awareness:** The inner landscape
2. **Situational awareness:** Reading the external environment
3. **Emotional intelligence:** Awareness of the emotional weather in yourself and others
4. **Systemic awareness:** Recognizing interconnected patterns

Each layer builds upon the other, creating a comprehensive navigation system for life's complex journeys, working in harmony, building a cohesive framework for understanding ourselves, others, and the world. Self-awareness is a foundation that grounds individuals in authenticity and anchors us to our core values. Situational awareness sharpens our ability to assess and engage with the external world and equips us to adapt to ever-changing contexts. Emotional intelligence strengthens our interpersonal connections, fostering connection and empathy. Finally, systemic awareness provides a broad and far-reaching perspective of interconnected systems, elevating perspective to the collective level.

Together, these layers create a dynamic system for understanding and engaging with the world, unlocking the tools to navigate routes and enabling us to approach life's complexities with greater clarity, insight, integrity, and purpose.

This multi-layered terrain is not static. It evolves as we grow, adapt, and deepen our understanding of ourselves and engage with the complexities of life. By continuously refining our awareness, we can better navigate our personal journeys and also contribute meaningfully to the larger systems of which we are a part. In embracing this multi-layered terrain of awareness, we empower ourselves to live with intentionality and connection, becoming both explorers and stewards of the world around us, forging a connection between the personal and the universal in the ever-expanding journey of life.

The blind spot phenomenon

Every explorer, every leader, every human has blind spots. These are the areas we cannot see, the unconscious patterns and assumptions that shape our decisions without our knowing. Included within this general realm is "inattentional blindness", the failure to perceive something in our visual field because we are busy focusing on something else. These have real-world implications, such as problems with distracted driving, workplace safety, making everyday decisions, and determining a market strategy.

When I worked as an executive advisor for the Pacific Crest Outward Bound School many years ago, I remember backpacking in the Oregon Cascades with a group that had varying levels of fitness and experience. As we hiked, two members of the group lagged further and further behind. I was aware of this, and yet simultaneously blind to the potential consequences as I assumed they would stay within sight. When weather conditions deteriorated, they became separated from the rest of the group. For a short while it seemed they had gotten lost in a very dense area of the forest, and it became a serious concern. The group agreed to a strategy to search and they were found without significant delay. There were no serious consequences. However, it was a good reminder to me of the need to stay aware of everything that is going on with oneself and others in an environment that may be unfamiliar to some, *and* to check my assumptions. Behind every blind spot there is usually an assumption that keeps our mind fixed and not curious.

With practice I have developed better situational awareness and learned to recognize blind spots. Which brings me to the point of saying, competence is not about being perfect. It's about being honest enough to see your flaws and know when you may be making choices that might endanger self and others. Practicing

> **Behind every blind spot there is usually an assumption that keeps our mind fixed and not curious.**

self-awareness transforms adventure and life itself from an external journey to an internal exploration. It has caused me to stay curious, remain flexible, and embrace uncertainty and continuous learning.

Benefits of self-awareness

Cultivating awareness can help us sense our emotional attachments and triggers before they send us spiraling into unconscious reactions. Awareness makes us more capable of loosening an emotion's hold on us. We reside more in choice and can discern appropriate responses, verbal or otherwise, in volatile situations. This is a vital benefit of awareness. Ultimately, the entire framework of self-realization and personal evolution depends upon it.

Consider this example: Maybe you tend to isolate or maybe you're stubborn. Have you noticed that you dislike these behaviors in others? Well, look in the mirror because we tend to attract people and situations that bring out that particular weakness in us. Does this dynamic happen because the universe wants to help us work through these things? Maybe. Is it karma? Possibly. Or is it just a fact of life that what we put out we get back multiple times over until we see what we're doing and change our behavior? All I know is that in my own life I've seen this dynamic at work many times. And it's never particularly fun. But once I became aware of what I was doing—of what wasn't working—I could change the pattern.

Cultivating awareness

Knowing about awareness is different from incorporating it into your daily life. Cultivating awareness requires significant introspection and contemplation. This means slowing down to practice mindfulness and being present to each moment. I'll say more about this when we get to Principle #8 on presence. Now, I want to point out that being as fully present as possible in the moment usually translates into understanding and better decision making.

Here are a few ways to develop better awareness of self, situations, emotions, and the environment.

The Three-Breath Practice

This simple yet powerful technique is used by many high-performance adventurers and leaders. It takes less than a minute and can transform your attitude in a meeting or your perspective in an uncomfortable interaction at work or at home. You can use it in any situation. For high stakes and consequential decisions, take more time, more breaths, and go to a much deeper level of contemplation.

1. First breath: Breathe in slowly; Notice your current state—emotional, mental, physical; exhale fully and slowly.

2. Second breath: Breathe in slowly; Observe your environment—physical, cultural, political; exhale fully and slowly.
3. Third breath: Breathe in slowly; Align your intention—keep your intention clear, not muddied by fear or limiting beliefs or emotional blocks; exhale fully and slowly.

The "Letting Go" Practice

True awareness requires continual release. Like a river constantly reshaping its course, we must be willing to let go of:

- Rigid expectations (which typically result in disappointment)
- Outdated narratives - (Has responding to my boss/spouse/partner/child/friend with this same narrative helped in the past? Or has it made things worse? What might an alternative narrative be?)
- Comfortable but limiting perspectives–(Has seeing people/situations/ideologies a certain way made me miss the magic of synchronicities, possibilities, and potential breakthroughs? Identify limiting beliefs and ask yourself - "If I shift that certain thought ... where do I end up? What is possible there"?)

Developing your Internal Compass

Emotional awareness is not about suppressing feelings but understanding them as valuable information. Think of emotions as internal GPS coordinates, offering guidance about our needs, boundaries, and potential.

A good practice for this is called "scanning." You slow down, take a breath and pay attention to what your body is telling you in that moment. The body can hold and telegraph emotions both positive or negative (even when we think we are hiding those emotions). Scan your body in situations that you are triggered or simply uncomfortable. Put your triggered thought aside for a moment. As you scan your body ask the question "Where am I feeling the _____?" (fill in the blank: angst, frustration, anger, sadness, disappointment, joy, anticipation; wonder, etc.) Wherever it is, take a deep breath and let the feeling go. See it leaving you.

This isn't about suppressing the emotion or pretending it doesn't exist. It is acknowledging that an emotion has grabbed you and is in charge of what you say or do next. That emotion is forcing a reaction and you are no longer in choice. Letting it go puts you back in charge. You now can choose how you want to respond in the moment.

Daily Reflection Journal

Start keeping a written journal, either handwritten or on your computer. Even if you only take five minutes to reflect and capture your thoughts and observations, it can be a tool to increase your awareness and help identify where you may be stuck. Writing also helps stuck emotions release.

Here are some prompts to get you started:

- What did I notice today that I hadn't noticed before about myself? About my relationships? My environment?
- What captured my attention today? Positive experiences? Problems? Issues? New things?
- What emotions colored my experiences? And why? Am I getting triggered? Am I in a repetitive emotional pattern that I want to keep? Or get rid of?

Sensory Awareness Meditation

This is the practice of "noticing what is." The challenge here is to keep our judgments, assessments, opinions and stories out of the noticing.

- Spend 10 minutes daily observing without judgment.
- Notice sounds, bodily sensations, thoughts passing through. Just notice, no judgments.

Perspective Shifting
- Regularly ask: "How might someone else see this situation?"
- Practicing empathy can be an awareness-expanding tool.

Tip:

Pick one or two practices and try them out for a week. Notice where you feel ease in the process and where you get hung up or frustrated. Just notice with no judgment. Review your day. Were you able to use a practice? Were there moments when using that practice could have helped? Just notice. Continue with these practices, or choose another one or two for the following week. And ... keep going.

PRINCIPLE #3

AUTHENTICITY: KNOW THY SELF, BE THY SELF

Be yourself; everyone else is already taken.

~ Oscar Wilde

Authenticity is not a destination, but a courageous journey of continuous self-discovery and self-expression. It is the profound art of living genuinely, being truly oneself, transcending social expectations, masks, and the protective layers we build to fit in or avoid vulnerability.

I learned a lot about authenticity during what turned out to be the first full successful descent of the Karnali River in western Nepal. An expedition that lasted just over two months, my role in this audacious group of nine river rats was as the re-supply coordinator. As such, I spent a lot of expedition time coordinating re-supply logistics, trekking to and from the locations where our gear was deployed.

A key reason the Karnali River had never been successfully run up to that point was because the extreme remoteness required extensive planning and logistics in getting people and gear to the river and out again. As well, it significantly amplified the risk. In case of an accident or death on the river, the nearest road and phone was at least a week's walk away—at times twice that. There were no mobile phones and very few available helicopters in those days, so airlift rescue was not a feasible option either.

Flying in on two chartered De Havilland Twin Otter planes from Kathmandu to Jumla in Western Nepal, before the planes landed on the grass runway it had to be cleared of goats and other animals. Unloading our gear, we were quite the sight to the locals who were both curious and amused. An area of tremendous beauty where some of the highest-altitude rice in the world is grown, we explored the region for several days waiting for local farmers to finish harvesting their fields before being available to help us carry gear on the week-long trek to the starting point on the river near the Tibetan border.

Because we were so far from the practical supports of civilization, team members were deeply reliant on each other. We each had our areas of expertise and responsibility, and our group's structure was that of a cooperative, which meant that there was no one leader. Decision making was by consensus. Our wellbeing—indeed our very survival—depended upon each of us being transparent and authentic with each other at all times at a level (and circumstances) none of us had ever experienced before.

For example, because the risk of injury and death was so high, one night around our campfire—huddled close to the flames for warmth, a breathtaking expanse of sky and stars above our heads—we talked about what we would do with the body if one of us died. There was no practical way we could pack out a body over treacherous territory over the course of weeks. So, after much somber discussion, we unanimously decided that the answer was to be buried somewhere along that river. High stakes consensus decision-making indeed! But our deep authenticity in behavior and actions with each other was one of the key reasons our expedition was successful and we all made it out alive.

Communal heart

Communicating across cultural boundaries presents an opportunity to build trust and make friends or create suspicion and division. Aside from the occasional missionary or anthropologist, the hamlets we passed on the river were populated with people who had seen very few outsiders in their lives because of the lack of roads in those days. Authenticity, spontaneity, and flexibility turned out to be helpful—even endearing—to strangers as much as to the core group. And the kindness and generosity evidenced by the villagers themselves were unforgettable.

Their isolation, the extreme weather, the mountains, the river itself—which was sometimes raging and challenging—had taught them that they had to nurture and support one another. And they extended that support to us without a second thought. Food in those places was not abundant, but they always unhesitatingly offered to share what they had.

Many have spoken about how long journeys tend to strip away pretense, forcing a deep, authentic engagement with oneself and the environment. The same was true for our group on that expedition.

Alignment

Many cultures and wisdom traditions equate authenticity with spiritual alignment - when one is in personal integrity and being true to one's inner spirit. A Zen proverb captures this beautifully: "Better to be a person of no rank than to be a false master."

Authenticity goes beyond mere factual honesty. It involves emotional honesty, acknowledging personal limitations, embracing one's complexity, and resisting the impulse to present a curated or idealized version of oneself—a temptation that is rampant in social media. Studies show that presentations of an idealized life as "perfect" without challenges or limitations have detrimental effects on both the person presenting the false picture and on others as well. Why? Because it's the complete antithesis of authenticity, which is the foundation of genuine trust.

> **When people consistently demonstrate alignment between words and actions, willingness to admit mistakes, genuine emotional presence, and transparent communication, they create an environment of psychological safety and deep connection.**

When people consistently demonstrate alignment between words and actions, willingness to admit mistakes, genuine emotional presence, and transparent communication, they create an environment of psychological safety and deep connection. Being vulnerable is not easy, but it is key to real authenticity. Brené Brown, American author of six number-one *New York*

Times bestsellers and a leading researcher on vulnerability, describes it as "the birthplace of innovation, creativity, and change."[7] Authentic vulnerability involves admitting mistakes, sharing genuine emotions, and being open to growth and learning.

The essence of authenticity at its core, encompasses several interconnected dimensions:

1. **Self-awareness**: Deep understanding of one's true values, emotions, and motivations
2. **Vulnerability**: Willingness to show one's true self, including imperfections and struggles
3. **Integrity**: Alignment between inner beliefs and external actions
4. **Honesty**: Truthful communication with oneself and others that is devoid of deception
5. **Courage**: Commitment to being genuine, even when it feels uncomfortable or risky

In professional settings, authenticity builds credibility and inspires confidence. Leaders who are authentic create a culture of transparency and psychological safety, empowering their teams to thrive.

Unfortunately, there are many modern challenges to unfettered authenticity. Some professional environments reward conformity. And the political climate in many countries does not lend itself to showing who you are or what you think or believe. Many millions do not have the luxury of total transparency and must consider their safety with every choice they make and each stand they take. Even so, when words and behavior align, commitments are kept, collaborative projects can come in under deadline, and the work product can be stellar. All these actions are authentic and can be conducted even under some of the most restrictive of settings.

As noted earlier, the increasing ubiquitousness of curated self-presentations on social media is very problematic. This practice exacerbates the internalized shame or self-doubt people have, as well as fears of judgment or rejection. The social media environment can also make it difficult for some people to discern between true and fake "authenticity." Understanding the difference is essential for making informed decisions about whom to trust and follow. It helps prevent falling victim to those who exploit their charisma or fame for personal gain to the detriment of others.

True authenticity is rooted in truthfulness and sincerity, and involves being transparent about one's intentions, actions, and beliefs. It means consistently aligning one's behavior with one's values, regardless of the situation or audience. In contrast, fake authenticity (an oxymoron if there ever was one) is a façade, a calculated image crafted to appear genuine while masking ulterior motives in order to gain approval, followers, or social status.

It is important to look deep and evaluate the actions and consistency of charismatic individuals. A truly authentic person will demonstrate integrity and honesty, even when it is inconvenient or unpopular. They will not change their core beliefs to fit in or please others. This is in contrast to those who may rely on their ability to charm in order to manipulate and deceive others.

> *"Don't listen to what people say, watch what they do."*[8]
> — Steven D. Levitt, Think Like a Freak

Practical pathways to cultivating authenticity

- **Self-Reflection Journaling**: Do regular, honest writing about experiences, emotions, and inner landscape
- **Mindful Communication**: Practice speaking from a place of genuine feeling
- **Boundary Setting**: Learn to say "No" and protect your true needs
- **Courageous Vulnerability**: Share struggles and imperfections with those you trust

These practices involve radical self-observation without judgment, and a recognition that our true nature is often obscured by ego, fear, and societal conditioning. Authentic individuals tend to experience higher self-esteem, more fulfilling relationships, increased resilience in the face of adversity, and reduced stress levels. Authenticity has been linked to enhanced creativity, improved problem-solving abilities, and a greater sense of purpose and meaning in life. By embracing our true selves, we unlock our full potential and live more fulfilling lives.

Conclusion

Authenticity is not about being perfect or comfortable. It is a courageous commitment to being real, embracing one's complexity, and living with integrity. In a world that often encourages conformity, authenticity becomes a revolutionary act of self-love, personal empowerment, and genuine human connection. I invite you to embark on a journey of authentic self-discovery. Challenge yourself to live in alignment with your values. Express yourself honestly and cultivate deeper connections with others. Remember, the world needs your unique voice and your authentic presence.

Reflective questions:

1. How often do you allow yourself to be truly vulnerable with others?
2. What masks do you wear to protect yourself from judgment or rejection? Is it with particular people? Is it with everybody?
3. Are your actions aligned with your core values and beliefs?
4. How can you cultivate more authenticity in your daily life?
5. What steps can you take to embrace your true self, imperfections and all?

PRINCIPLE #4

RESIDE IN CHOICE

It's not what happens to you, but how you react to it that matters.

~ Epicitus

The ability to consciously reside in choice marks the difference between being at the mercy of circumstances and being the author of one's own story. And I learned this lesson early on.

A couple months before my 12th birthday I went on a backpacking trip in the Adirondack mountains in upstate New York with our small local scout troop in Pennsylvania. I was excited to be climbing Mt. Marcy, the highest mountain in New York, exploring the beautiful wilderness in that area. It was the biggest adventure of my life to that point, and I was thrilled to have the opportunity to do this. And yet, as one of the two youngest boys on the trip, it wasn't easy to keep up with the older kids who were stronger and could hike much faster. Dealing with the reality of it was arduous, and after many grueling days of difficult effort taking me to the point exhaustion, I found myself asking myself *What am I doing here? Why am I going through this?*

It was a pivotal moment. One where I could have easily slid into victim mode and made myself and everyone else miserable for the rest of the trip. Instead, from some "older than my years" place deep inside, the thought arose: "*I chose this.*"

No one had forced me to be where I was. To the contrary, filled with enthusiasm, I'd begged my parents to let me go into those mountains to explore new territory. If it wasn't easy, if I wasn't enjoying myself in that moment, I had no one to blame but myself. The realization picked me up by my boot straps. And while the rest of the trip remained physically challenging, at least my mind and emotions were on board and not adding to my troubles!

Over the years, on other adventures, I continued to apply this highly self-responsible, self-empowering orientation to the point that I knew that if I got hurt or died on one of my self-chosen adventures, no one else would really be at fault. If I made miscalculations in my preparation and my equipment needs, if I underestimated how easy or hard the effort would be, I was 100 percent responsible for whatever happened and how I felt about it along the way.

Eventually, this became a way to think about other challenging situations in relationships, in working within organizations, and life in general. And, as I completely embraced full responsibility for whatever I was engaged in, I became a much better adventurer and human being. I became happier and more successful in all the endeavors I attempted.

Don't get me wrong. I'm not "perfect" at this. I don't always remember to fully embrace the "choice-ness" of a situation as my first reflex. I'm still working on that, and sometimes it takes a while to come around to it. Sometimes it requires a reminder from my wife or someone else. However, when I do get to the point of getting fully grounded in the reality that I am 100 percent responsible and fully in choice, it always results in a substantial shift where 1) I feel happier and am in a better mind-frame to take needed action steps; 2) I make better life decisions after integrating the lessons from the situation; and 3) I am nicer to be around.

Shifting mindset

The Roman philosopher-emperor, Marcus Aurelius, wrote in his *Meditations*: "You have power over your mind, not outside events. Realize this, and you will find strength."[9] In alignment with this truism, one of the most practical applications of residing in choice is the shift from "have to" to "get to" thinking. This simple linguistic change reflects a profound opportunity when we get that most obligations represent privileges when viewed from a different perspective. We don't "have to" attend a challenging meeting, we "get to" show up, be challenged, and contribute to important decisions. We don't "have to" face difficult tests, we "get to" grow through overcoming them.

This shift isn't mere positive thinking, it's a recognition of reality. The very fact that we can make choices, face challenges, and take action represents a privilege to many. As Viktor Frankl, holocaust survivor and psychiatrist, observed in his book *Man's Search for Meaning*, "Everything can be taken from a man but one thing: the last of the human freedoms—to choose one's attitude in any given set of circumstances, to choose one's own way."

Practical benefits and implementation

The benefits of residing in choice extend far beyond philosophical satisfaction. Research in psychology and neuroscience increasingly supports what wisdom traditions have long taught: conscious choice-making enhances everything from stress resistance to decision quality to leadership effectiveness.

Studies in organizational behavior show that employees who perceive greater autonomy and choice in their work demonstrate higher engagement, creativity, and job satisfaction. Leaders who actively practice and promote choice-consciousness tend to build more resilient, adaptable teams.

Some practical steps for developing this capacity include:

- Regular reflection: Take time daily to identify choices, even in seemingly choice-less situations. What aspects remain under your control? What responses are available?

- Language awareness: Notice when you use "have to" language and experiment with reframing situations in terms of choice and opportunity.

- Decision journaling: Keep a record of key choices and their outcomes, building awareness of your choice-making patterns and their consequences.

- Responsibility practice: When facing challenges, ask "What am I choosing here?" rather than "Why is this happening to me?"

Navigating difficult choices

Sometimes residing in choice means choosing between difficult options or accepting short-term discomfort for long-term benefit. The mountaineer who chooses to turn back despite being close to the summit, the leader who chooses to have a difficult conversation rather than avoid conflict, the activist who chooses to face arrest in service of a cause—all demonstrate that residing in choice doesn't mean choosing the easy path.

Perhaps no one has demonstrated the power of choice in extreme circumstances more profoundly than Austrian psychiatrist Viktor Frankl. Along with his family, during World War II he was sent to the Nazi Thereseinstadt concentration camp where his father died of starvation and pneumonia. Transported to Auschwitz in 1944, he was present when his mother and brother were sent to the gas chambers. Transferred again to the Bergen-Belsen camp, Frankl lost his wife to typhus. Post-war, in his seminal work *Man's Search for Meaning*, Frankl related how even in the most dehumanizing conditions imaginable, there remained what he called "the last of human freedoms"—the ability to choose one's attitude toward suffering. "Between stimulus and response there is a space," he wrote. "In that space is our power to choose our response. In our response lies our growth and our freedom."[10]

> "Between stimulus and response there is a space." "In that space is our power to choose our response. In our response lies our growth and our freedom."
> ~ *Viktor Frankl*

Adventure Mindset

Stripped of everything—possessions, family, dignity, and basic human rights—he could still choose how to meet and carry his suffering. Instead of falling prey to victimhood and dehumanization, he chose to find meaning in his experience. Frankl observed fellow prisoners, despite starvation and abuse, give away their last piece of bread to others who needed it more. He witnessed acts of compassion and nobility that demonstrated how human beings can rise above the most unimaginable cruelty. He sustained his balance by helping fellow prisoners find hope and reasons to live by mentally reconstructing destroyed manuscripts, and by imagining giving lectures about the psychological lessons learned in the camps.

We don't need such an extreme example to show the power to choose our responses even when all other choices are taken away. In other challenging circumstances, we see similar examples. Like wartime POWs creating tap codes to communicate with each other, choosing to maintain human connection and mental acuity despite isolation. Or cancer patients moving through their fear or anger or despair, to choosing to view their illness as an opportunity to deepen self-understanding, relationships, and an appreciation of life. Or a teen who loses out on an opportunity, acknowledge their disappointment then chooses to appreciate their courage in taking the risk in the first place. They know they are so much more than this one situation. There is so much more awaiting them.

The key insight from all of these examples is that choice exists in how we frame and interpret events. It resides in the meaning we assign to our experiences and the direction of our attention. How we relate to our own suffering, and what values we choose to express even in restrictive circumstances is vitally important.

> *"Choose to be optimistic. It feels better."*
> ~ the Dalai Lama XIV

Upleveling your choice-consciousness

There is the notion in Buddhism and some other spiritual traditions, that pain can be separate from suffering, and that suffering can be a choice. As the Dalai Lama put it: "Choose to be optimistic. It feels better." This isn't naive positivity, but a recognition that even our emotional responses involve choice. You can practice this in everyday situations to make the skill accessible in extreme circumstances. Some practical approaches include:

- **Response pause**: Deliberately take a pause between stimulus (trigger) and response, even if just for a breath, to recognize the choice point
- **Meaning-making**: Actively choose what meaning to assign to difficult situations
- **Attention direction**: Consciously choose where to focus your attention, even in adverse circumstances
- **Values connection**: Identify ways to express core values even within severe constraints
- **Perspective shifting**: Practice finding different ways to view challenging situations

Conclusion

Residing in choice represents both an ancient wisdom and a crucial skill for modern life. Whether navigating the basic challenges of daily life or leading an expedition across Antarctica, the capacity to remain conscious of, and grounded in, choice marks the difference between being a victim of circumstances and being the author of one's life story. Like any worthy adventure, developing this capacity involves challenges, setbacks, and moments of doubt. Yet also, like any worthy adventure, the rewards—increased resilience, better decisions, stronger leadership, and deeper satisfaction—make the journey worthwhile. And each day presents new opportunities to practice, new challenges to navigate, and new chances to choose who we become.

Reflective questions

Think of a situation where you feel you "have to" do something. What shifts in your perspective when you reframe it as "I choose to" or "I get to"? What values or commitments are you honoring through this choice?

1. Recall a time when you consciously chose your response to a difficult situation rather than reacting automatically and it made a difference in the interaction. What enabled you to access that choice point? What were the impacts of your chosen response versus what might have happened with an automatic reaction?

2. In your current work or life situation, where do you feel most constrained or "choice-less?" Looking

deeper, what choices actually remain available to you in terms of your response, attitude, or meaning-making around these situations?

3. In your own leadership or influence roles, where do you have opportunities to help others recognize and access their power of choice? What prevents you from doing this more often?

4. Looking at your daily routines and habits, which ones do you do mindlessly versus consciously choose? How might bringing more choice-consciousness to these routines change your experience of them?

PRINCIPLE #5

VALUES: THEIR ROLE IN DECISION-MAKING & ORGANIZATIONAL SUCCESS

Values are like fingerprints. Nobody's is the same, but you leave 'em all over everything you do.

~ Elvis Presley

The world of adventure and exploration provides rich examples of how values guide decision-making in high-stakes situations. Consider the previously mentioned case of Alex Honnold, the free solo climber who made history by ascending El Capitan, a 3000-foot vertical rock formation in Yosemite National Park, without ropes or traditional safety harnesses. His success depended, not just on physical skill but on a rigorous decision-making process grounded in clear values around preparation and safety, and meticulous attention to detail, honesty, brutal self-assessment, and courage balanced with prudence. Or Polish mountaineer Wanda Rutkiewicz, the first woman to reach the summit of K2 and the third woman to summit Mount Everest. Her exploits clearly demonstrated how personal values of independence and calculated risk-taking could be balanced with team responsibility, enabling her to turn back from summiting attempts by overriding summit fever and ego.

But heroic adventures don't just take place on a cliff face. Just as a mountaineer must balance ambition with prudence, organizations and the people who lead them must balance growth with sustainability, innovation with stability, and individual achievement with collective success.

Silicon Valley Bank was still a startup when Ken Wilcox joined it in 1990. In April 2001 he became CEO of SVB just in time for the worst recession in the history of American technology. First came the dotcom crash, then communications companies and most tech companies followed. In his book *Leading Through Culture: How Real Leaders Create Cultures That Motivate People to Achieve Great Things*, Ken writes about his years as CEO, 2001-2011[11] and how he and the company survived the economic cycle and tech industry slump. Indeed, the company thrived during his tenure because of his focus on building a culture of shared values.

I watched Ken's leadership style firsthand and saw how he motivated people to achieve great things. And he did it primarily because he understood the importance of creating a value-based culture in the workplace. "Values are the bedrock of culture," he says. "Values are shared norms. It is of the utmost importance that your team shares common values ... for they act as a North Star, enabling a group of people to know, in most cases intuitively, if at any given time they're pointed in the right direction.

"Values are not just the glue that holds an organization together, they give it a unique sense of identity. Values also allow an organization to become more or less self-governing. They are also the 'voice of the conscience' that enables your employees to know what to do, even when their leaders are not around."

The universal nature of values

Like the North Star that has guided explorers for millennia, our core values provide direction, purpose, and meaning to our journey through life and our interactions with others. Across cultures and throughout history, human societies have developed systems of values that guide behavior and decision-making. In Buddhist philosophy, the Noble Eightfold Path provides a framework for ethical living based on values such as right understanding, right intention, and right action. The ancient Greek philosopher Aristotle, in his *Nicomachean Ethics*, emphasized the importance of virtue (arête) in leading a fulfilling life. He argued that virtues are not merely theoretical constructs but practical guides for action that must be cultivated through practice.[12]

Different cultures approach values and decision-making in distinct ways, yet certain distinctive patterns emerged over time. East Asian traditions tend to emphasize harmony and balance, long-term thinking, collective welfare, and respect for hierarchy and experience. Western traditions have tended to emphasize individual rights and responsibilities, innovation and change, merit-based achievement, and systematic analysis. Indigenous traditions often emphasize connection to nature, intergenerational responsibility, holistic thinking, and community consensus. These traditional tendencies are changing as different cultures interact with each other and learn from one another.

On that paddling descent of the Karnali River in Nepal I talked about in the last section, the cultural values of the people in the tiny villages we met on that journey were easily observed. Mutual support, generosity, concern for the well-being of others (including strangers), and a willingness to be of service. Clearly shaped by the harsh, isolated environment they lived in, these were the unspoken values these people held dear and lived by. And as strangers in their midst, we were grateful for them!

In his book *Human Universals*,[13] anthropology professor Donald Brown at the University of California, Santa Barbara identified certain values that appear to be present across all human cultures, including:

- Fairness and reciprocity
- Truth-telling and disapproval of lying
- Love and attachment
- Cooperation and group loyalty
- Protection of the vulnerable
- Respect for wisdom and experience

These universal values emerge from our shared human experience and the requirements of social living. And, although they may seem to be related to and supported by the ethics espoused by various religions, as the Dalai Lama notes in his book *Ethics for the New Millennium*, "What we need today is an approach to ethics which makes no recourse to religion and can be equally acceptable to those with faith and those without: a secular ethics."[14]

Consider the example of Fridtjof Nansen, a remarkable Norwegian explorer, scientist, and humanitarian who left an indelible mark on the world. His life was a testament to a unique blend of personal and cultural—indeed universal—values, including a dedication to intellectual curiosity, physical courage, and deep compassion. Nansen led the first crossing of Greenland's interior in 1888 at the age of 26 and later made his most famous and daring expedition on his ship "Fram," which he designed to drift with the Arctic ice, gathering invaluable scientific data on Arctic currents and conditions. After World War I, Nansen dedicated himself to humanitarian work, playing a crucial role in repatriating prisoners of war and aiding refugees displaced by conflicts. Nansen had a strong sense of duty to humanity and was known for his integrity, courage, and compassion. His dedication to helping those in need earned him the Nobel Peace Prize in 1922.[15]

Organizational applications

American management consultant and organizational behavior expert Margaret "Meg" Wheatley points out in her 2006 book *Leadership and the New Science,* "Organizations are living systems, not machines. Like all living systems, they are self-organizing networks of relationships."[16]

As with any other human cultural creation, values play a crucial role in any organizational endeavor. They act as filters through which we process information, evaluate options, and make choices. The alignment between individual and organizational values has become increasingly recognized as a critical factor in both personal and organizational success. Jim Collins, an American researcher, author, and consultant who focused on business management and company sustainability and growth, found that companies with strong, well-articulated core values significantly outperformed their competitors over the long term, especially when individual and organizational goals were in alignment, along with shared values.[17] Indeed, research shows that modern organizations and companies with strong value alignment with their employees show:

- 33 percent higher employee engagement
- 27 percent lower turnover
- 40 percent higher customer satisfaction

American political scientist, economist, sociologist, and Nobel laureate in economic science, Herbert Simon, introduced the concept of "bounded rationality," recognizing that human decision-makers must rely on values and heuristics to make choices in complex environments.[18] Decisions are limited to the information they have, with their values being the lens through which they see the situation.

The decision-making process typically involves:

- Problem recognition
- Information gathering
- Alternative generation
- Evaluation of alternatives
- Choice

- Implementation
- Review

And yet, each stage of the above decision-making process is grounded in values that influence each step—how we define what constitutes a problem, how we determine what information is relevant, evaluate options, generate acceptable alternatives, and finally implement solutions.

The relationship between values and decision-making becomes particularly relevant when we consider Complexity Theory and Chaos Theory. Belfast-born economist W. Brian Arthur, a friend of mine, argues in his book *Complexity and the Economy,*[19] that economic systems, like other complex adaptive systems—including mountain climbing and general exploration—exhibit emergent properties that cannot be reduced to simple cause-and-effect relationships. In such environments, values serve as "strange attractors," organizing principles that help create coherent patterns within apparent chaos.

AI—the new frontier

If ever there was a human adventure profoundly impacting every aspect of culture and civilization, it is our entry into the treacherous waters of partnership with artificial intelligence. The initial values-based question "Should we go there at all?" has long past reached its "sell by" date. As AI systems become more sophisticated, penetrating every aspect of human life from security and privacy to economics to art and entertainment to space exploration to medicine, questions regarding which human values to embed into algorithmic computing processes and how to incorporate them are becoming increasingly urgent.

As American complex systems scientist and entrepreneur J. Doyne Farmer, Director of Complexity Economics at the Institute for New Economic Thinking at the Oxford Martin School in the UK points out, to produce beneficial outcomes, implementing AI requires developing robust value frameworks. "The challenge is not just to make AI systems smart," he says, "but to make them wise."[20]

But making AI "value-aligned" with humanity presents several challenges. The first is "value specification." How do we precisely specify human values in machine-readable form?

The second hurdle on this adventure is "value learning." How can AI systems learn and adapt to human values over time? Lastly comes "value consistency." How do we ensure AI systems maintain value alignment as they evolve?

Like any adventure, implementing value-alignment in this area is going to require:

Risk assessment and management
- Thorough preparation
- Balance of ambition and safety
- Transparent communication

Adaptive leadership
- Flexible tactics within firm values
- Inclusive decision-making
- Crisis management grounded in principles

Values: Their Role in Decision-Making & Organizational Success

Clear articulation of values
- Explicit statement of core values
- Regular discussion and renewal
- Connection to strategic objectives

Stakeholder consideration
- Impact on team members
- Effect on local communities
- Environmental consequences

Cultural respect
- Cross-cultural bridge building
- Integration of local knowledge and traditional wisdom
- Responsible documentation

Systematic integration
- Alignment of policies and procedures
- Integration into evaluation systems
- Recognition and reward systems

Leadership example
- Visible commitment to values
- Consistency in decision-making
- Transparency in processes

Long-term perspective and legacy
- Knowledge sharing, mentorship and education
- Sustainable practices
- Inspiration for future generations

Regular reassessment
- Monitoring of alignment
- Feedback mechanisms
- Adaptation as needed

Just as an explorer must balance ambition with safety, the journey with AI must balance growth with sustainability, innovation with stability, and technical achievement with collective "success," which is nothing less than the healthy future of all humanity.

Conclusion

Values serve as our compass in navigating both personal and organizational challenges. Like the experienced mountaineer who must make critical decisions in changing conditions, successful organizations and individuals must ground their decision-making in strong values while remaining adaptable to changing circumstances.

As we face the challenges of our time—from climate change to technological disruption to political tumult—our success will depend not just on our technical capabilities but on our ability to make decisions guided by strong values and ethical principles. In this context, the lessons from adventure, ancient wisdom, and modern organizational theory converge to show us a path forward: one that combines courage with wisdom, innovation with tradition, and individual achievement with collective responsibility.

Reflective Questions

1. Think of a time when you made a decision that didn't feel right, even though it seemed logical. In retrospect, which of your values might have been trying to guide you?

2. Consider a team or organization you are part of: How explicitly are values discussed and used in decision-making? What opportunities do you see for better integrating values into daily operations?

3. What role do values play in how you handle failure or setbacks? Are there values that help you maintain resilience and perspective during challenging times?

4. How do your values influence the way you build and maintain relationships, both personally and professionally? Are there values you'd like to express more fully in your relationships?

5. Think of someone whose decision-making you admire. What values do their choices seem to reflect? How might you incorporate similar principles into your own decision-making process?

PRINCIPLE # 6

COMMUNAL SELF-RELIANCE: THE POWER OF COLLABORATIVE INTERDEPENDENCE

In the long history of humankind (and animal kind, too) those who learned to collaborate and improvise most effectively have prevailed.

~ Charles Darwin

In an increasingly fragmented and individualistic world, communal self-reliance emerges as a powerful antidote to social isolation, economic inequality, systemic disconnection and stress. Communal self-reliance is not about complete independence, but rather about creating robust, supportive networks that enable individuals and communities to thrive. It represents a holistic approach to social organization that recognizes our fundamental interconnectedness and the immense potential that emerges when people work together with genuine respect, empathy, and shared purpose.

Deep collaboration transcends mere transactional interactions. It is a profound commitment to understanding and supporting the genuine needs, aspirations, and potential of all involved parties. This approach requires a radical shift from competitive mindsets to cooperative frameworks that recognize the inherent value of each individual's contribution. When we truly collaborate, we move beyond zero-sum thinking. Instead of viewing interactions as win-lose scenarios, we begin to see opportunities for mutual growth and collective advancement. This perspective acknowledges that the success of one does not necessitate the failure of another, but can instead create expansive possibilities for everyone involved.

> **The success of one does not necessitate the failure of another, but can instead create expansive possibilities for everyone involved.**

Historically, one of the most notable examples of communal self-reliance and leadership excellence is the Antarctic expedition Anglo-Irish explorer Sir Ernest Henry Shackleton led in 1914-16. In the early 20th century, when most exploration was defined by individual heroism and personal glory, Shackleton authored a different story—a narrative of collective survival that would become a seminal case study in leadership, teamwork, and human resilience for decades to come.

Odyssey of survival

When Shackleton began the Imperial Trans-Antarctic Expedition in 1914, his ambition was to make the first land crossing of Antarctica. His crew selection process was revolutionary.

Communal Self-reliance: The Power of Collaborative Interdependence

He didn't just choose the most physically capable men, but those who could also maintain psychological stability under extreme stress. His famous recruitment advertisement—rumored to read "Men wanted for hazardous journey. Low wages, bitter cold, long months of complete darkness, constant danger, safe return doubtful. Honor and recognition in case of success."—was more than a recruitment call. It was the character statement of a man bidding kindred spirits to join him on a journey like no other.[21]

They sailed to Antarctica in late 1914 and in January 1915, their ship *Endurance* became trapped in pack ice. For 10 months, the crew was stuck onboard until the ship was ultimately crushed by the ice and destroyed. This left them stranded almost a thousand miles from the nearest human settlement. Pulling whatever equipment they could salvage from the ship, the men camped on the ice. As the winds howled across the endless white expanse of Antarctica, the men faced what seemed like certain doom. Finally, after months surviving on the ice, Shackleton and five crew members embarked on an 800-mile journey to Elephant Island in a 22-foot salvaged dinghy across the most treacherous ocean on the planet to seek help.[22]

Their navigation impeccable, their resolve unbreakable, after 16 days sailing, they reached South Georgia Island and then trekked across its mountainous interior—a route never before attempted. Staggering into the small port outpost, they were able to get a larger boat and supplies to go back to rescue the others.

Against all odds, every single member of the expedition survived. When they were finally rescued in August 1916, they had spent 497 days in one of the most inhospitable environments imaginable. One and all, they emerged transformed.[23]

Collective resilience

The 1914 Imperial Trans-Antarctic Expedition became one of the most extraordinary tales of human collaboration and resilience in exploration history. Imagine being stuck on the ice, temperatures plummeting to minus 40 degrees, with nothing but your teammates between you and certain death. In such moments, respect isn't a courtesy—it's oxygen. Contempt, judgment, argument, selfishness, hopelessness ... these were fatal weaknesses that would unravel the most carefully created human network faster than the coldest Antarctic wind could freeze exposed skin.

But Shackleton understood survival wasn't about individual heroism but rather about nurturing collective will. Throughout the 22-month ordeal, he adhered to the key leadership principle that could best ensure survival: everyone matters. When food was scarce, he commanded equal distribution. When morale dropped, he became a psychological architect, understanding that hope was a team's most valuable resource. He recognized that the mental state of each crew member affected the entire group's chances of survival. Once they had to leave the ship and began camping on the ice, Shackleton is reported to have requested to sleep in the tents of the most disgruntled crew members. Because of this, he had a deep understanding of all the problems being faced by them and the rest of the crew.[24]

Thus, Shackleton transformed potential conflict into collaborative problem-solving, turning what could have been a tragic expedition into a legendary tale of human endurance.

Reflections for today's leaders

As crew member Frank Worsley later wrote, "Shackleton's sangfroid and resourcefulness seemed to grow with the danger."[25] He didn't just lead a successful expedition, he created a blueprint for human collaboration under extreme conditions. His leadership was not about commanding, but about creating a living, breathing organism capable of adapting, supporting, and ultimately triumphing.

In an era of increasing complexity, technological disruption, and global challenges, Shackleton's approach is highly relevant for today's organizations. Leadership is no longer about individual brilliance but about creating ecosystems of mutual support, rapid adaptation, and shared purpose. The *Endurance* expedition teaches us that our greatest resource is not technology, strategy, or individual talent—but our capacity to work together, to see beyond immediate self-interest, and to transform seemingly insurmountable challenges into extraordinary achievements.

Shackleton's lessons for modern organizations

- **Relationship is paramount**

  Organizations that create environments where colleagues feel safe to take risks, voice concerns, and support each other outperform those fixated on individual metrics.

Adventure Mindset

- **Leadership is about building relationships**
  Modern leaders must abandon the heroic, lone-wolf model and embrace a more interconnected approach.

- **Emotional intelligence is key**
  Shackleton understood that survival was 90 percent psychological. He meticulously managed the crew's morale, creating routines, organizing entertainment, and ensuring that no one felt left behind or dispensable.

- **Transparent communication**
  He held daily meetings, keeping everyone informed about their situation. No secrets, no hierarchy-driven information hoarding. Every crew member understood the collective challenge.

- **Equitable treatment**
  Rations, workload, and hope were distributed equally. No special treatment for officers, no marginalization of junior members. In today's application, leaders and team members must both be able to receive and deliver constructive feedback/criticism. Individuals who would raise criticisms of leadership need to know that their earnest dissent/suggestions will be respected. Confrontation, often perceived negatively, can actually be a powerful tool for growth when applied equitably and approached with respect and genuine curiosity.

- **Resolve conflicts**
  Effective conflict resolution involves understanding diverse perspectives through active listening and

finding common ground. (Sleeping in the same tent.) Maintaining emotional regulation and focusing on shared objectives. By reframing confrontation as an opportunity for mutual understanding and collective problem-solving, communities can transform potential sources of division into moments of deeper connection and innovation.

- **Meet challenges with flexibility**

    Organizations that can rapidly reorient around emerging challenges—rather than clinging to original plans—will thrive in volatile environments.

- **Diversity is strength**

    Shackleton's crew included men from different backgrounds, skills, and temperaments. Their diversity was not a challenge to manage but a resource to leverage. The same is true for any organization.

- **Continuous motivation matters more than occasional inspiration**

    It's easy to be motivated during exciting moments. Shackleton's genius was maintaining team spirit during months of monotony and seeming hopelessness.

- **Ego-based competition is a dangerous game**

    The zero-sum game—where one person's gain is another's loss—is a dangerous illusion. In real-world expeditions and organizations, true progress happens when we view challenges through a lens of mutual growth. Imagine a team approaching a complex problem not as a battle to be won, but as a puzzle to be solved together.

- **Respect is the foundation of healthy collaboration**
Respect creates trust, openness, and communication, and creates meaningful engagement. It transforms potential adversaries into allies into and converts competitive conflicts into collaborative opportunities.

Beyond the "tragedy of the commons"

Modern technological and economic landscapes have dramatically transformed our concept of "commons." Some spaces once considered public are now controlled by private, for-profit entities. Social media platforms, communication networks, and digital spaces that were once conceived as open, democratic forums have become commodified environments driven by engagement metrics and advertising revenues. This privatization of public spaces poses significant challenges to genuine community collaboration, creating environments that often prioritize algorithm-driven engagement over meaningful human connection.

Much of this privatization has been deemed inevitable because the classic "tragedy of the commons" narrative suggests that shared resources are predictably depleted when some people overuse those resources even while others exercise voluntary restraint, resulting in a "tragedy" for all concerned. However, contemporary research challenges this pessimistic view. American political scientist and political economist Elinor Ostrom's work on economic governance of the commons was awarded the Nobel Memorial Prize in Economic Sciences. It reveals that communities can indeed effectively manage shared resources through, 1) clearly defined boundaries, 2) collective decision-making, 3) graduated sanctions for misuse, 4) conflict resolution mechanisms, and 5) nested governance structures.[26]

The tragedy of the commons is not an inevitable fate but a failure of imagination. Over the years I've seen and been a member of outdoor equipment cooperatives, food co-ops, and other cooperative support organizations that worked very well. One memorable community resource I benefited from was a "tool library" formed by a community in Eugene, Oregon in the late 1970s. Just like a book library, one could borrow from the collection—a hammer, a drill, or most any other tool one would need for doing basic carpentry, masonry, and other construction or repairs, then return them for the next person to use. In those days, most tools, especially power tools, were expensive items. This tool library was a fabulous community resource that was not abused and benefitted everyone.

Other systems that reward cooperation and collective stewardship include community land trusts, community-based resource management systems and indigenous management practices that maintain sustainable resource systems through practices that embed stewardship values and create social rewards for responsible management.

> *The tragedy of the commons is not an inevitable fate but a failure of imagination.*

Human beings innately desire connection. Traditionally this need has been filled by having strong connections with our neighbors, strong bonds with people we gather with to worship, or to play sports, or do other activities, and a strong sense of local belonging fostered by community-based activities. But as the modern media landscape has evolved, its algorithms have drawn us more and more into 'virtual' communities that have caused us to have less and less in common with our physical neighbors, and thus we experience less connection and understanding. Which has resulted in a vast loneliness and sense of unsafety for the majority.

The greatest adventure

But we aren't fated to be left out on the ice, alone, to fend for ourselves. The innate human desire for safety, and the capacity for deep collaboration that can ensure such safety, is growing globally. The transition from individualized, competitive, zero-sum thinking to positive-sum thinking represents a much-needed fundamental paradigm shift. Instead of viewing resources and opportunities as fixed and scarce and something to be battled over, a positive-sum perspective recognizes the generative potential of collaborative approaches. And it all starts by creating a sense of shared purpose—a compelling, meaningful objective that transcends individual interests.

Would I be exaggerating to suggest that, like Shackleton's crew, the survival of many organizations and institutions, as well as the wellbeing and lives of most of humanity, now depend upon such a paradigm shift? When individuals align their personal growth with broader human goals, extraordinary achievements become possible. But this alignment requires clear communication of human values, transparent decision-making processes, opportunities for meaningful contribution, recognition of individual and collective efforts, and mechanisms for feedback and continuous improvement.

There needs to be a commitment to continuous learning and individual and collective growth. We need to create an environment where everybody feels safe expressing ideas, perspectives, and vulnerabilities. There needs to be both individual and collective responsibility for adherence to values and outcomes.

This communal self-reliance is not a utopian ideal but a practical approach to addressing complex social, economic, and environmental challenges. By cultivating deep collaboration, mutual respect, and a genuine commitment to collective well-being, we can create more resilient, adaptive, and fulfilling communities. Yes, the path forward requires a collective reimagining of our potential—moving from fragmented individualism toward a more integrated, supportive, and generative way of living and working together. But peace and international cooperation is both vital and achievable.

If humanity is to survive and thrive in the coming generations, we will need to reinvent our adversarial systems as we know them today. Our greatest adventure is learning to truly collaborate—to recognize that in the most fundamental sense, we're all in this together, and that when people work together, miracles can and do occur.

Reflective questions

1. How do you truly feel in your mind, heart, and gut, about continuing to support a zero-sum approach in the workplace? In the rest of your life?
2. Have you had an experience of genuine collaboration that "raised the bar" for everyone involved? That culminated in unexpectedly positive results?
3. Are you willing to engage small, intentional practices that can help you cultivate positive sum interactions? Such as:
   - Seeking to understand another before being understood
   - Listening more than you speak
   - Creating spaces where diverse perspectives are valued
   - Developing win-win negotiation skills
   - Prioritizing long-term relationships over short-term gains
   - Celebrating collective achievements

PRINCIPLE #7

EMPATHY AND COMPASSION: THE CORNERSTONE OF HUMAN CONNECTION

If you want others to be happy, practice compassion.
If you want to be happy, practice compassion.

~ Dalai Lama

Empathy is the ability to understand and share the feelings of another, to step into someone else's shoes and truly comprehend their emotional landscape. While the *expression* of empathy and the compassion that follows may vary across cultures, it appears to be a nearly universal human trait and value. This suggests that empathy is not just a learned behavior but potentially a fundamental aspect of human neurological and emotional architecture. Compassion motivates us to take action to alleviate the suffering we sense and provide support.

Three types of empathy exist: cognitive empathy, emotional empathy, and compassionate empathy. I find these distinctions helpful for people to discern the level or type of empathy that is customary for them, as well as the type they may want to strengthen. In a nutshell:

- Cognitive empathy is understanding the other person's thoughts, feelings, and perspective; "To see how they see it."
- Emotional empathy is experiencing the same emotions as the other person is feeling.
- Compassionate empathy combines understanding and feeling with a desire to help; being motivated to take action.

These powerful qualities transcend cultural boundaries, philosophical traditions, and personal differences, offering a universal language of understanding that has the potential to transform individual lives and entire societies.

Practical benefits

Creating a deep, meaningful connection with another person recognizes our shared humanity.

In the realm of exploration, developing the capacity for empathy and compassion can literally save your life. Imagine getting into a two-person kayak to navigate a huge rapid or hooking up to climb a vertical cliff face with a partner who is scared and uncertain of their ability to perform adequately. Being able to emotionally "read" the situation and then compassionately and directly address critical concerns is paramount for the safety of all concerned.

Leaders who have an interest in creating team collaboration and an environment that empowers people to make decisions to take action, who want team members committed to bringing their best to each opportunity, would do well to strengthen their own skills of empathy and compassion. Empathetic leadership has been shown to increase team cohesion, improve communication, and drive innovation. When individuals feel understood and valued, they are more likely to take creative risks, collaborate effectively, and maintain high levels of motivation. In conflict resolution, empathy becomes a powerful tool. By genuinely understanding different perspectives, we can move beyond defensive positions and find mutually beneficial solutions. As the saying goes, "Seek first to understand, then to be understood."[27] This approach can transform potential confrontations into opportunities for mutual growth and understanding.

In personal relationships, empathy acts as a healing force. It allows us to create deeper connections, validate each other's experiences, and provide meaningful support. By practicing compassion, we create safe emotional spaces where vulnerability is welcomed and understanding is cultivated. Research shows that individuals who regularly engage in compassionate practices report lower stress levels, improved mental health, and greater overall life satisfaction. It's a powerful reminder that compassion is not just a gift to others, but a profound act of self-care.

Speaking of self-care, I'm sorry to have to say it, but sincerity is an essential quality of

> **In personal relationships, empathy acts as a healing force. It allows us to create deeper connections, validate each other's experiences, and provide meaningful support.**

true empathy and compassion. Unfortunately, there are some people who put on a show of empathy and compassion in a cynical attempt at manipulating others for malevolent purposes. While rare, fake empathy can be employed as a clever tool to get people to do things, and is useful in the current media environment to get more attention. Sometimes it may not be easy to initially detect this particular application of inauthenticity. However, it tends to be revealed over time when actions may not be congruent with words spoken.

Mirror mirror

Modern neuroscience has discovered the neurological basis for empathetic connection in the form of what are termed "mirror neurons." When we observe someone experiencing an emotion, mirror neurons in our brains fire, giving us the same feelings as if we were experiencing the emotion ourselves. (This is why commercials can sometimes make us cry or break out in a fit of laughter!) And the good news is, developing true empathy is a skill that can be consciously cultivated. We can help promote this brain activity by employing active listening, suspending judgment, asking thoughtful questions, and genuinely trying to understand different perspectives. Meditation practices, particularly loving-kindness meditation, have been scientifically proven to enhance empathetic capabilities as well.

Every major spiritual and philosophical tradition emphasizes the importance of empathy and compassion. In Christianity, Jesus's commandment to "Love one another as I have loved you" (John 13:34) represents a profound call to empathetic connection. Buddhist teachings speak extensively about compassion, with the concept of "karuna" representing active compassion and the desire to relieve suffering. In Judaism, the concept of "chesed" (loving-kindness) emphasizes compassionate action as a fundamental spiritual practice. The Islamic tradition similarly highlights mercy and compassion, with the *Quran* repeatedly describing Allah as "the Most Gracious, the Most Merciful."

Hinduism's concept of "ahimsa" (non-violence) is deeply rooted in compassion, encouraging practitioners to minimize suffering for all living beings. People of other faiths, such as the Taoists, Jains, Bahá'í, followers of Zoroaster, and others, are all aligned in this, as are indigenous people who recognize that empathy is not just a moral choice but a recognition of our fundamental unity. Native American philosophies, for instance, emphasize the importance of walking in another's moccasins—a literal metaphor for empathy that predates modern psychological understanding.

Shared Humanity

Empathy and compassion represent more than moral virtues—they are essential skills for navigating our increasingly complex, interconnected world, where cultures can collide and fear is stoked. The behaviors of empathy and compassion remind us of our shared humanity, transcending differences of culture, belief, and experience. By choosing to practice empathy, we not only support others but also enrich our own lives. We create more meaningful, supportive, and understanding communities. In a world often characterized by division and misunderstanding, empathy and compassion offer us a powerful alternative—a path of connection, healing, and mutual understanding.

Reflective questions

1. Have you had the experience of sensing someone's emotional state, even though they may have been trying to keep it hidden?
2. Have you experienced someone sensing that you were keeping your emotions hidden? How did it make you feel when they inquired or offered support?
3. Can you see the personal and social benefit of being able to "walk in another's shoes?"
4. Imagine the relief of understanding why someone is the way they are instead of simply being put out or annoyed by their "issues." Can you see how that ability could improve the quality of your relationships and your own life?

PRINCIPLE #8

CULTIVATE PRESENCE

People who feel empowered by your presence become kindred spirits.

~ Wayne Dyer

In the rush of modern life, with its constant distractions and endless demands for attention, the concept of presence—of being fully engaged in the current moment—has emerged as both an ancient wisdom and a crucial skill for contemporary success. Presence is more than simply being physically located in a particular place and time. It represents a state of complete awareness and engagement with the current moment, unmarred by regrets about the past or anxieties about the future. This quality of attention brings with it a remarkable power—the power to see clearly, to respond appropriately, and to connect deeply with our experiences and those around us.

Adventure Mindset

Traditional approaches

Across cultures and throughout history, wisdom traditions have emphasized the importance of presence. The Buddha taught that the present moment is the only moment in which we can truly live, learn, and transform. In Japanese culture, the concept of "ma"—the meaningful space between things—relates closely to presence. The tea ceremony, for instance, is designed to cultivate the attainment of complete presence in every gesture.

Perhaps one of the world's most lucid descriptions of presence comes from the mystic philosopher and spiritual teacher George Ivanovich Gurdjieff. Born in the Russian Empire in 1866 (in what is now Gyumri, Armenia), Gurdjieff taught that ordinary human consciousness is a state of "waking sleep" where we falsely believe we're present while actually being lost in mechanical thoughts and reactions. True presence, which he called "self-remembering," requires maintaining simultaneous awareness of our physical sensations, emotional state, thoughts, external environment, and, most crucially, awareness of oneself as the observer of all these elements.[28]

He emphasized that this state demands intentional effort and cannot arise automatically. Unlike simple concentration, self-remembering involves a comprehensive attention, with awareness directed both outward at activities and inward at oneself. While such moments of genuine presence may be brief, Gurdjieff said they generate a different quality of energy and consciousness that can accumulate over time, especially when practiced during daily activities rather than just in meditation.[29]

Surely, you have noticed when somebody with a commanding presence enters a room? They stand out. They literally emanate what can only be called "power." All heads turn towards them. Even though they may say nothing and seem to do nothing, they draw attention. That's presence.

Modern German-born spiritual teacher Eckhart Tolle describes it this way: "When you are present, when your attention is fully in the Now, Presence will flow into and transform what you do. There will be a quality and power in it. When your attention moves into the Now, there is an alertness. It is as if you are waking from the dream of thought, the dream of past and future. Such clarity, such simplicity lies in the Now. Your deeper self behind or underneath thought, as it were. You feel a conscious presence."[30]

Of course, the world's great adventurers and explorers have long understood the crucial importance of presence. When climbing a difficult pitch or navigating treacherous waters, anything less than complete attention to the present moment can be fatal. As legendary American rock climber Carolynn Marie Hill has noted, "When you're climbing at your limit, you're not thinking about anything else. You're not even thinking about climbing. You just are."

Similarly, Norwegian explorer, author and politician Erling Kagge, who has completed the "Three Poles Challenge" (North Pole, South Pole, and Mount Everest), speaks of how presence in extreme environments creates a unique clarity: "In these moments of complete presence, when survival depends on each decision, you discover what truly matters. The mind becomes quiet, and wisdom emerges from that silence."[31]

> "In these moments of complete presence, when survival depends on each decision, you discover what truly matters. The mind becomes quiet, and wisdom emerges from that silence."

The science of presence

Modern research has begun to validate what ancient traditions have long known. Studies in neuroscience show that mindfulness practices such as yoga, meditation, and qigong are techniques for cultivating presence that can literally reshape the brain, enhancing neural networks associated with attention, emotional regulation, and decision-making while reducing brain activity in areas associated with anxiety and mind-wandering.

The work of researchers like Richard Davidson, professor of psychology and psychiatry at the University of Wisconsin-Madison has demonstrated that regular mindfulness practice can lead to increased activation in the prefrontal cortex, an area associated with positive emotions and resilience, thus making it a practical tool for enhancing well-being and performance.

In the book *Presence: Human Purpose and the Field of the Future*, author Peter Senge, founding chairperson of the Society for Organizational Learning and a senior lecturer at MIT, and his co-authors Otto Scharmer, Joseph Jaworski, and Betty Sue Flowers, examine how change happens and discuss the development of a new theory about change and learning that is heavily dependent upon the nature and importance of presence.[32]

The authors describe presence as "a state of 'letting come,' of consciously participating in a larger field for change." This perspective suggests that presence is not merely a passive state but an active engagement with the potential that exists in each moment. The book introduces several key concepts that are perhaps even more relevant today than when first published in 2004, what the authors call the "deep learning cycle." This cycle involves three movements:

- Sensing: Becoming one with the world
- Presencing: Connecting to the source of the highest future possibility
- Realizing: Acting swiftly, with a natural flow

One of the book's crucial insights is the importance of "**suspending**" our habitual ways of thinking and seeing. This means temporarily letting go of our assumptions and mental models to see reality with fresh eyes. Like letting go of our belief that we can be checking email or social media on our phone and be fully engaged with people in the room with us—or better yet while driving our car in traffic.

In today's world of information overload and algorithmic echo chambers, this capacity becomes increasingly vital. The authors emphasize the practice of "**redirecting**" attention from external objects to the process of perception itself. This meta-awareness helps us understand not just what we're seeing, but how we're seeing it, revealing our blind spots and biases.

Like a climber on a cliff face suspended a thousand feet above the ground, the authors describe the importance of "**letting go**" old ideas, thoughts, identities, and ways of operating. This involves releasing our attachment to familiar patterns and being willing to exist in the Now in a state of "not knowing"—a capability essential for adaptation and innovation. Following the letting go is a process of "**letting come**"—allowing new possibilities to emerge naturally rather than mentally calculating and forcing solutions. This requires cultivating a kind of alert patience and trust in the process of emergence.

The authors describe how new possibilities, once sensed, begin to "**crystallize**" into clearer intention and vision. This isn't about traditional strategic planning, but rather about allowing clarity to emerge from deep presence while engaging quick, experimental action—"**prototyping**" as a way to learn and adapt in real time. This involves maintaining presence while testing new approaches and remaining open to feedback. Finally, the authors discuss how new ways of operating can become embedded in larger systems and structures, always while maintaining the flexibility that comes from presence.

Particularly relevant today is their discussion of the "social field"—the totality of connections, relationships, and possibilities that exist in any human system. In our hyperconnected world, becoming aware of, understanding, and working with this field has become essential for effective leadership and change-making.

Finding presence in nature

One of the most interesting approaches to gaining presence is taught by my friend and teacher, John Milton. As mentioned previously, John is a pioneering ecologist and spiritual teacher who has studied and worked with many spiritual lineages. He founded The Way of Nature, developing wilderness programs and unique methods to help people connect deeply with nature and their own inner sense of self, presence, perception, and knowing.[33]

Through solo experiences in remote wilderness areas, spending time alone in nature—often for extended periods—program participants often develop what Milton calls "natural knowing." They access a direct, unmediated perception of reality that transcends ordinary awareness—an awareness that sometimes includes enhanced sensory awareness, intuitive knowledge of natural processes, and deep insights into their life purpose that transforms their relationship with the natural world and their understanding of their place within it.

In my own work with John, I've learned how presence is not just an abstract concept but a natural human potential that our modern lifestyle tends to suppress. That potential can be reawakened through proper practice and guidance. The many times I've gone solo into nature have been profound experiences. Of course, finding time to spend a week (or several weeks) sitting quietly by myself in nature has not always been easy. However, it has always been rewarding taking a complete break from all of life's "normal" distractions, especially the electronic tethers. "The less you take with you, the more that awaits you," John always said. And I've found this to be true. In the quiet of nature, we are more able to hear the inner voice or what has been called the "still small voice" within. And that which arises from within can include a wide array of experiences and aspects of reality: a sense of bliss, real stillness, awareness of self beyond the ego, non-dual oneness, and more.

Cultivating presence

As you can see, the benefits of cultivating presence obviously extend far beyond the spiritual realm. Research has shown that greater presence can lead to enhanced decision-making capabilities, improved leadership effectiveness. increased creativity and innovation, greater resilience in facing challenges, reduced stress and anxiety, improved relationship quality, and even better physical health outcomes

> **Presence serves as an antidote to fragmented attention**

Moreover, presence serves as an antidote to fragmented attention—what many consider the defining challenge of our time. In an era of constant digital distraction, the ability to be fully present has become both more difficult and more valuable. Here are a few suggested methods of cultivating presence:

- **Mindful breathing**: Simply bringing attention to the breath serves as an anchor to the present moment.
- **Body awareness**: Regular practice of body scanning and movement awareness helps ground attention in the present moment through physical sensation
- **Intentional pausing:** Creating deliberate spaces between activities (even between each bite of food) allows for fuller engagement with each moment rather than constant rushing from one thing to the next.

- **Nature Connection**: Time in nature, where the mind naturally quiets, provides an ideal environment for developing presence. A great example is the Japanese idea of *shinrin-yoku*, which translates as "forest bathing" or "taking in the forest atmosphere."
- **Mindful Communication**: Practicing full attention in conversations, truly listening rather than simply waiting to speak.

The present is a gift

The word "present" carries a double meaning—it refers both to the current moment and to a gift. This linguistic connection hints at a deeper truth: the present moment is indeed a gift, offering possibilities for growth, connection, and transformation that exist nowhere else.

As we face increasingly complex challenges in both our personal lives and our organizations, the capacity for presence becomes not just nice-to-have but a practical necessity. Whether we're scaling literal mountains or metaphorical ones, presence provides the foundation for wise action and meaningful achievement. In cultivating presence, we don't just enhance our performance or well-being—we open ourselves to the full richness of life itself.

Reflective questions

1. When in your life have you felt most fully present? What were the conditions that enabled this state, and what impact did it have on your life and your effectiveness?

2. When was the last time you spent time alone in nature? What was your experience? Was it difficult? Rewarding? Too quiet? What was your response to the quiet?

3. What are your biggest barriers to being present? Beyond external distractions, what internal patterns, fears, or habits pull you away from the present moment?

4. What practices or conditions help you return to presence when you notice you've become scattered or disconnected? How might you build more of these into your daily routine?

5. How does your relationship with the natural world affect your capacity for presence? What experiences in nature have taught you about being present?

6. If you were to make presence a primary practice in your life for the next three months, what would need to change? What benefits do you imagine might emerge, both personally and professionally?

PRINCIPLE #9

EQUANIMITY: STILLNESS WITHIN

Even a happy life cannot be without a measure of darkness, and the word happy would lose its meaning if not balanced by sadness. It is far better to take things as they come along with patience and equanimity.

~ Carl Jung

Equanimity: the ability to maintain inner equilibrium regardless of external circumstances.

Hold that thought.

Several years ago, I was climbing Mt. Rainier, the 14,410' active stratovolcano in the Cascade Range of the Pacific Northwest that lies southeast of Seattle, Washington. Known to local Native American tribes as Tahoma, "the mother of waters" or "frozen water," the mountain is also honored as the "Grandmother Mountain that continually feeds the people." It last erupted in 1894-95.

On that climb, I remember approaching a section where the glacier had fractured into a series of massive cracks, creating a labyrinth of crevasses, their blue-green depths partially

Adventure Mindset

concealed by recent snows. My mind drifted to the 125 climbers who had died in the last hundred years climbing this mountain, some of them near this very spot. I thought about a good friend who had died on another Cascade peak not far from this one. I felt my heartbeat quicken as I heard, like whispers on the wind, not warnings but reminders: *The mountain does not care about your fear or your courage. It responds only to your choices, your technique, your ability to remain present* ... but kept my breathing steady. Finding equanimity, that delicate balance between awareness of danger and surrender to fear, I acknowledged these ghosts with reverence, then intentionally let them go.

> **The mountain does not care about your fear or your courage. It responds only to your choices, your technique, your ability to remain present ...**

Fear was information, not a command. I assessed the crevasses carefully, noting the wind-packed surfaces and edges dropping off at distinct angles. My mind cataloged the variables without emotional interference—the overnight temperature, the recent snowfalls, the time of day, the weight of our team going through the crevasse field. Each step required full attention as I proceeded upward, one careful step after another. The crampons on my boots bit into the hardpack with reassuring firmness, but I kept my ice axe ready to plunge into the snow with the swift, powerful self-arrest motion needed if one of us slipped. I mentally rehearsed the gear and technique we would use for rescue from a crevasse if one of us fell in. Not with

> **Fear is information, not a command.**

anxiety, but with the calm acceptance that preparation was our best defense against catastrophe.

We continued upward, each step a mindful negotiation with the mountain. In the realm of ice and gravity, there was no room for either panic or complacency—only the balanced awareness that would allow us, with luck and skill, to get safely to the summit and back home again. [... so we could be *talking* about this great adventure!]

Universal wisdom and the necessity of equanimity

The essence of mountain wisdom I've learned over years of climbing is this: No matter the situation, panic consumes energy and clouds judgment. Calm observation preserves both. Equanimity isn't the absence of fear or danger, but rather the ability to maintain inner equilibrium regardless of external circumstances.

> **Equanimity isn't the absence of fear or danger, but rather the ability to maintain inner equilibrium regardless of external circumstances.**

Since time immemorial, this state of mental and emotional balance has consistently separated those who succeed from those who falter. In Buddhism, equanimity is described as the factor that maintains balance between faith and wisdom, energy and concentration. The characteristic of conveying evenness of mind with its function being to see things impartially, the Buddha taught that equanimity was essential for true wisdom, saying, "Looking at life as it is with perfect equanimity, the mind becomes still." In Stoic philosophy, the concept appears as "ataraxia," a state of tranquil composure independent of external circumstances.[34]

Surely it was "ataraxia" that allowed the Mars Rover team at NASA to successfully navigate the nail-biting "seven minutes of terror" during the Perseverance rover's landing at Mars' Jezero Crater February 2021. Despite years of preparation and billions of dollars at stake, the team maintained the collective composure that enabled clear decision-making during the critical landing phase. No doubt afterwards the NASA team would have appreciated Italian author and mountaineer Reinhold Messner's words: "In the death zone, emotions are lethal. One must maintain perfect balance between action and acceptance."

The neuroscience of equanimity

As I write this, we face daunting global challenges and change happening at mind-bending speeds. The adventure of life demands no less than our full presence and balanced engagement, making equanimity not just a noble aspiration but an essential skill for modern living and wellbeing.

No surprise, research shows that regular meditation and mindfulness practices associated with cultivating equanimity lead to increased gray matter density in brain regions associated with emotional regulation, attention, and decision-making. Studies published in the *Journal of Neuroscience* and elsewhere have demonstrated that long-term meditators show reduced activity in the amygdala, the brain's fear center, when presented with scary emotional stimuli, leaving the prefrontal cortex responsible for executive function and decision-making free to operate optimally, unimpaired by the stress response that might otherwise cloud judgment.[35]

A path to equanimity

Jon Kabat-Zinn, has a PhD in molecular biology from MIT, and focuses his research on mind/body interactions for healing and on the effects of mindfulness-based stress reduction (MBSR) on the brain, body, and immune system. He is professor emeritus of medicine and the creator of the Stress Reduction Clinic and the Center for Mindfulness in Medicine, Health Care, and Society at the University of Massachusetts Medical School. He started this work in 1979, when consciousness studies were barely a blip on the radar screen of the western world.[36]

Mindfulness is the practice of being fully present in the moment with an open, non-judgmental awareness, paying attention to your thoughts, emotions, and physical sensations while embracing them with acceptance and compassion. Intention sets the practice into motion, and meditation helps its cultivation. Recognized widely as an essential tool for developing presence and equanimity, Kabat-Zinn notes, "You can't stop the waves, but you can learn to surf." A metaphor that perfectly captures the essence of equanimity (not the absence of challenges but rather the skilled response to them), Kabat-Zinn recommends approaching mindfulness this way:

- **Perspective shifting**: Regularly consider multiple viewpoints and realize the impermanence of all things to help grow your mental flexibility characteristic of equanimity.

- **Physical movement:** Yoga, Tai chi, mindful walking, and other mindful movement helps integrate bodily awareness with emotional balance creating a foundation of steady presence that supports equanimity in challenging situations.

- **Contemplative reflection:** Regular consideration of our emotional triggers and attachments helps us understand their origins and reduce their power over us. An "evening review" of our actions and thoughts throughout the day gives us time to notice our patterns and unrealized attachments to certain outcomes, etc.

- **Mindfulness meditation:** Regular practice in observing thoughts and emotions without attachment or aversion builds the capacity for equanimity. Start with short daily sessions of focused breathing, gradually extending duration and complexity.

- **Repetition is key.**

Most high-stress, high-risk professions supply rigorous training to ensure skill and composure in the face of adverse events such as what pilots Chesley "Sully" Sullenberger and Jeffrey Skiles faced a few years ago when US Airways Flight 1549 struck a flock of birds shortly after takeoff from LaGuardia airport in New York. Both men exhibited stunning composure as they made the swift decision to glide the plane to a water landing on the Hudson River near Midtown Manhattan. As Sullenberger later wrote: "One way of looking at this might be that for 42 years, I've been making small, regular deposits in this bank of experience, education, and training. And on January 15, the balance was sufficient so that I could make a very large withdrawal."[37]

Organizational applications

In modern organizations, equanimity becomes increasingly valuable as complexity and uncertainty rise. Leaders who maintain composure under pressure create psychological safety for their teams, enabling better performance, decision-making, and innovation in others. Research in organizational behavior at the Center for Creative Leadership shows that teams led by individuals with high emotional equilibrium demonstrate:

- 37 percent better decision-making under pressure
- 58 percent improved conflict resolution
- 45 percent higher innovation rates
- 62 percent better stress management

Buddhist teacher Thich Nhat Hanh explains the phenomenon this way: "When you are solid and stable, you can generate peace and joy for the people around you." This ripple effect makes equanimity not just an individual virtue but a collective resource.

Other practical benefits are:

- Enriched relationships: Equanimity creates space between stimulus and response, enabling more skillful, harmonious interactions.

- Better health: Reduced stress reactivity supports improved immune function and cardiovascular health.
- Greater resilience: The ability to maintain perspective in difficulty supports faster recovery from setbacks.

Reflective Questions

1. Consider a pattern in your life where your own emotional reactivity consistently creates challenges. How does this pattern serve you? (What's the perceived benefit?) What price do you pay for maintaining it? What would become possible if you could approach these situations with greater equanimity?
2. Think about your relationship with uncertainty. When do you find yourself most strongly grasping for control? What beliefs or fears drive this grasping? How might developing greater equanimity change your relationship with uncertainty?
3. Think about a significant change or challenge your organization is facing. What emotions are driving current responses to this situation? How might approaching it with greater equanimity reveal options or possibilities that anxiety or resistance are currently obscuring?
4. Consider your leadership style (whether formal or informal). How does your emotional state influence those around you? What would become possible for your team if you could maintain steadier equanimity during high-pressure situations?

5. Are there key areas of your life where things could be more of what you want them to be? What patterns of behavior or emotional attachments are connected to these areas? What are possible lessons you are being invited to learn?

NOTE: This reflection process itself is an opportunity to practice equanimity. Notice any judgments that arise about your responses and practice holding them with gentle awareness rather than self-criticism.

PRINCIPLE #10

PREPARED SPONTANEITY

Creativity arises out of the tension between spontaneity and limitations, the latter (like the riverbank) forcing the spontaneity into the various forms which are essential to the work of art or poem.

~ Rollo May

Prepared spontaneity is about finding the right balance of thorough preparation developing strong foundational skills with the ability to improvise when that is called for. The old wisdom of "Hope for the best, prepare for challenges" seems to apply here.

When I backpacked through remote mountainous terrain (Himalayas, Andes, Rockies, and other North American mountains, etc.), I learned that when one is carrying everything on one's back for weeks on end, each item in the bag must be strategically chosen. One hopes that those things that are excluded will not sacrifice safety, health, or any other aspect of effectiveness or success of the journey.

Items that can be used for more than one purpose tend to be valued more highly. For example, on his solo circumnavigation of the Arctic Circle, South African-born explorer Mike Horn used the same equipment for different purposes. Depending on conditions, he used his ski poles to help traverse snow and ice, then used them as tent supports at night, and as fishing rods for ice fishing when conditions permitted, demonstrating resourceful simplicity in action.

There have been times when I've been in expedition situations where I did not have the right equipment, or the equipment I had was impaired, and it became life-threatening. Several times the threat to my life was serious hypothermia, and one of those times was on the Karnali River in western Nepal. We were about three weeks into that expedition and had passed the midpoint. Like most rivers in the Himalaya, the water temperature can be very cold. Most of the Karnali had been snowmelt just a few days before, and the water temperature was about 40 degrees Fahrenheit / 4 Celsius.

Although the river was getting bigger with each tributary we passed, the gradient was diminishing as the topography opened a bit more. While the risks were still high, we felt the river was becoming a bit easier as we continued downstream. We'd also had a nice stretch of sunny days, which helped us stay warm—which was particularly good for me because I'd had an issue with my wetsuit gear earlier on. One morning, however, greeted us with heavy overcast and clouds. Of course, it was that day that my kayak flipped a bit more often in the rapids I was paddling. Each time I promptly righted myself with a classic Eskimo roll. I was wet and chagrined, but had no choice but to keep going.

Now, seriously cold water has a way of sapping your strength, and as time went on I felt my energy draining as I flipped in another rapid. And then another. And then another. Each time I righted myself more slowly. And the more time I spent upside down in the water, the colder and weaker I got. By the time we stopped for a break, I'd already gone past the shivering stage of hypothermia and my condition was becoming serious. My fingers and other peripheral areas were numb and, as I climbed out of the kayak at the water's edge, I staggered and slipped, barely able to climb the bank. My speech was slurred and my cognitive functions had also declined significantly. Fortunately, the other members of the team recognized the symptoms and took the actions needed to save my life. We had to adjust our plans for the day, but we were prepared for such emergencies, and everybody flexibly pitched in without the slightest hesitation.

Successful adventurers always have to remain open to unexpected changes. Alison Hargreaves, the first woman to solo climb Everest without supplemental oxygen developed a method of "progressive adaptation," gradually building experience while maintaining flexibility in timing and route selection. She developed a comprehensive understanding of weather patterns and her own physiological responses, allowing her to make crucial real-time decisions during her ascents. Her approach to high-altitude climbing offers valuable lessons for both adventurers and leaders of organizations alike. Whether scaling a rockface or a company, climbing their highest peak or reaching for the most audacious goals, prepared spontaneity is a winning strategy.

A different kind of tool

But perhaps, one of the most essential tools to have in the prepared spontaneity tool kit isn't even physical. It's having a knack for out-of-the-box thinking. We can't anticipate every unexpected change, new obstacle, or sudden shift in the landscape. What we can do is build our "prepared spontaneity" muscles by 1) increasing our comfort with divergent/out-of-the-box thinking; 2) learning to question our own assumptions; and 3) being ready to pivot when those assumptions no longer apply.

Out-of-the-box thinking will surely require questioning assumptions—yours and your team's, as well as norms that have become habitual rather than intentional, and unexamined, unspoken expectations.

I get caught in my own assumptions all the time. Think about the times you have been so certain that you knew what would or would not be acceptable, workable, possible. Think about the assumptions that led you to think that. Now imagine that you began to question what you knew to be so—at least what you thought you knew to be so. Do you think anything could have been different—about the process, the outcome, the relationships involved?

A quick check-in on assumptions that I sometimes use goes like this:

1. I identify my assumption
2. I ask myself: Do I know this to be true? (I usually say YES!)

3. I ask myself: Do I <u>really</u> know or do I just think I know? (This is when the internal conversation begins to hedge ... *Well, um, I thought I knew* ...
4. The "I just think I know" response is my cue to thoroughly check out the assumption, the person, the team, the research, whatever.)

Just-in-time spontaneity

I recall a friend of mine telling the story of how she planned a two-week solo car trip around Chile. Trouble was, she didn't speak a word of Spanish. She struggled even to remember the Spanish words for "left" and "right." (derecha / izquierda.) But one of her assumptions was that her rental car would have GPS because, well, just because.

It wasn't until after she'd rented the car that had no GPS (assumption no longer applies ...) and gotten out on the road that she grasped the difficulty of her situation. She had her computer with her and could research places to stay and even make the reservation. Road signs kept her moving in the right direction enough to get her to a specific village in the middle of nowhere. But she realized that this was where her lack of Spanish could be a problem. How was she ever going to find the place when she got to the village? Who could she ask if she couldn't speak the language?

But then came the "aha"—the out of the box thinking. She realized that every village had a central square. And at every central square there was always at least one local taxi driver. So, when she got to a village she'd drive to the square, find a driver, show him the address of her destination and pantomime paying him to drive to the address while she followed in her car. It worked like a charm, and her two-week travel adventure in Chile went off without a hitch.

Complexity theory

Complex adaptive systems, like successful expeditions or organizations, exhibit emergent behavior—patterns that arise from the interaction of multiple elements rather than from central control. Most experienced adventurers have some level of understanding of complexity theory and approach expedition challenges by creating frameworks that allow for spontaneous adaptation rather than trying to control every variable.

This concept, which balances thorough preparation with the ability to adapt and improvise holds valuable lessons for modern endeavors. Yvon Chouinard is an accomplished climber and founder of the famous outdoor equipment company, Patagonia. As a young climber in the 1950s, he noticed that much of the equipment on the market was poorly made and damaging to the environment, especially the climbing hardware being used at the time. So, Chouinard taught himself blacksmithing and started fashioning reusable climbing hardware out of steel. Not only did he use them himself, he sold them to fellow climbers, thus providing himself with an income to keep his climbing career going.

One item led to another, and soon Chouinard found himself running an ecofriendly outdoor equipment business before the word "ecofriendly" had even been coined. Over and over Chouinard spontaneously introduced or changed product lines. His out-of-the-box thinking led him to create fleece jackets and insulating garments made from recycled materials. He switched to organic cotton for Patagonia's more mainstream clothing lines. He made sure the company gave employees flexible hours so they could spend time outdoors, pursuing their sporting passions, surfing, paddling and hiking.

The essence of Chouinard's success is the meeting of his adventure spirit with his values—protecting the environment, respect for people and their well-being, their ideas and their work. He also wanted to make it easy and comfortable for the adventurer or the weekend warrior to experience nature. He created new technologies to solve problems or fill a need, not allowing perceived limitations or assumptions to negate possibility. The company became a global leader demonstrating the viability of a whole new economic shift in commercial thinking supporting the triple bottom line of "people, planet, and profits."

Steve Jobs' approach to product development at Apple reflected similar principles to Chouinard's. While maintaining rigorous technical standards, Jobs built in flexibility to pivot based on new technologies and market feedback. The development of the iPhone, for instance, began as a tablet project before adapting to changing market opportunities.

Ray Dalio, the American founder of the hedge fund Bridgewater Associates, an asset management firm focused on delivering unique insights and specialty partnership for global institutional investors, combines systematic analysis with adaptable decision-making processes, creating what Dalio calls "radical transparency." A system that's both robust and highly responsive to changing conditions, it's also a firm dedicated to radical transparency. Rigorous in their respect for one another, demanding integrity in word and deed, as well as open contribution to the conversation—all of this is a way of being for people in the firm. A way of being that is highly supportive of prepared spontaneity.

Companies like Toyota have built their success on the concept of "lean manufacturing" which incorporates many elements of prepared spontaneity—minimal waste (making it easier to pivot), flexible response to changing conditions, and continuous improvement through learning from challenges. Anywhere along the design process, in product development, even on the assembly line, a person can "stop the line" with concerns about product integrity, safety, or component viability without fear of retribution. This is prepared spontaneity in action.

Personal application and skill development

The old military adage that "no plan survives first contact with the enemy" reflects the reality that all complex endeavors require adaptability. However, this doesn't negate the value of planning. As President Dwight D. Eisenhower noted, "Plans are worthless, but planning is everything."

How to develop prepared spontaneity? As you can imagine, it's difficult due to the almost antithetical nature of what we're talking about. But it helps to realize that preparation is basically about building capabilities that allow for effective response to changing conditions. Here are a few suggestions to aid in developing this approach:

- Build a broad base of knowledge and experience
- Develop fundamental skills to automaticity
- Understand underlying principles rather than just specific techniques
- Regular practice in varying conditions
- Mental preparation for uncertainty and change

Remember what the ancient Stoic philosopher Seneca said when he advised, "Luck is what happens when preparation meets opportunity."[38] In today's world, those who can master the art of prepared spontaneity, building strong foundations while maintaining the flexibility to adapt, will be best positioned to thrive in an increasingly complex and changing environment.

Reflective questions

1. How do you currently balance thoroughness with flexibility in your planning process? Are there areas where you might be over-planning or under-preparing? What would better balance look like?

2. Consider a challenging goal you're working toward. What different pathways could lead to success? How might you prepare for multiple scenarios while staying focused on the core objective?

3. How does your team currently handle unexpected challenges? What patterns emerge in successful versus unsuccessful responses?

PRINCIPLE #11

INSPIRATION AND VISION 1.0

The truly successful person inspires others to do more than they have thought possible for themselves.

~ Denis Waitley

Like a spark that ignites a flame, inspiration has the power to awaken dormant potential, fuel perseverance, and illuminate paths previously shrouded in darkness. Whether scaling mountain peaks, leading organizations, or pursuing personal visions, inspiration serves as both catalyst and sustaining force for human achievement and fulfillment.

It makes sense that the original root of inspiration—inspire—means "spirit within," because many of the great inventions and breakthroughs over history seem to have come through some form of communion with spirit or source consciousness. For example, the Greek scholar Archimedes reputedly shouted "Eureka!" ("I have found it!") as he realized he'd discovered a method to determine the purity of gold by watching the water get displaced as he got into a bathtub. Or how about Thomas Edison? After testing no fewer than 6,000 materials that didn't work well enough or burn long enough to secure a patent on his design, Edison's vision of replacing dangerous candles and oil lamps with an electrical lighting source remained only a vision until it "hit" him one day to try carbonized bamboo as a filament. Afterwards Edison famously stated that his work was "Ninety percent perspiration, 10 percent inspiration." Certainly, this dynamic is in evidence with all the brilliant innovators I've seen in Silicon Valley and elsewhere. A lot of people work very hard, putting in the perspiration. They may have a vision that guides and draws them, but without inspiration as a key ingredient, nothing truly creative or innovative ever happens.

Inspiration and vision in the world

Transcending cultural boundaries, both inspiration and vision appear as a central theme in wisdom traditions worldwide. In Buddhist philosophy, "Right View" (Sammā Ditthi) forms the first step of the Noble Eightfold Path, emphasizing the importance of seeing things as they truly are while maintaining a clear vision of where one's path leads. The Dalai Lama often speaks of vision as integral to spiritual development, stating, "In order to carry a positive action we must develop here a positive vision."

In Hindu tradition, the third eye chakra (Ajna) represents inner vision and wisdom, highlighting the deep connection between spiritual insight and the ability to perceive future possibilities. The Bhagavad Gita teaches that "Where there is no vision, there is no hope," emphasizing the intrinsic link between clear sight and purposeful action. Indigenous

Inspiration and Vision 1.0

cultures worldwide have developed sophisticated practices around vision and its role in personal and communal development. Perhaps none is more well-known than the Native American vision quest, a rite of passage that continues to resonate with modern seekers. During these solitary journeys into nature, individuals fast and pray, seeking personal vision and purpose. Among the Lakota, the Hanblecheya (crying for a vision) ceremony represents a profound understanding that clear vision comes through challenge and sacrifice.

Like two sides of the same coin, vision and inspiration draw us onward and upward toward a new adventure and a new way of being. They take turns leading the way ... sometimes a grand inspiring idea strikes first, and it creates a new vision and pathway for us to follow.

> *Like two sides of the same coin, vision and inspiration draw us onward and upward toward a new adventure and a new way of being.*

On a trip to a developing country, we're inspired by local school children working on a project to create cheap solar-powered cook stoves for families in the bush without electricity. We jump at the chance to join the project, bringing onboard financial and technical aid from our country. From the original inspiration a vision takes hold of a joint educational program between kids in our two countries focused on each other helping solve local community needs. And from there the project grows.

Sometimes the opposite happens. A vision builds in us quickly or slowly—a new creation such as a new kind of bicycle that can navigate both land surfaces and water. The vision of such a creation inspires us to proceed—to gather the tools and materials to build this "water bike." Or, if we're not the mechanical type, to find people who can help us bring our vision to light. We find inspiration along the way. A comment from someone or an internal flash of insight fire us anew, galvanizing us to stay steadfast on our path.

Vision and inspiration work together in a "chicken and egg" kind of relationship. But why do I call the vision described in this principle "Vision 1.0?" It's because Vision 1.0 is practical. It aims at providing a solution to a down-to-earth need that can be personal, like having the vision of owning a home, or having a prosperous retirement. Or it can be a vision of something to create that will benefit others. Either way, it's a vision of something that can be done—perhaps with great difficulty, but it's based upon an idea that can be directly put into motion. As to what Vision 2.0 is ... we'll talk about that closer to the end of this whole adventure!

Lighting the torch

The impact of inspiration can be clearly seen in organizational and collaborative settings, where collective achievement depends on shared vision and sustained motivation. When collaborative colleagues are genuinely inspired, they transcend mere compliance and enter a state of committed engagement where their work becomes an expression of purpose rather than obligation.

For example, Reshma Saujani, an American lawyer and politician, identified a critical gap in the tech industry and moved to change it by founding the organization Girls Who Code, challenging tech industry norms and legitimizing women working in the male-dominated field of computer technology. In the world of adventure and exploration, inspiration comes hand in glove with the many "firsts" that have changed humanity's view of both our world and human potential. May 20-21, 1927, American pilot Charles Lindbergh brought nations closer together when he made the first nonstop flight from New York to Paris in his plane, the Spirit of St. Louis, flying alone for 33.5 hours over a distance of a distance of 3,600 miles. British runner Roger Bannister became an overnight legend when he broke the "unbreakable" four-minute mile May 6, 1954, changing humanity's view of what the human body can do forever.

Adventurers like Sylvia Earle constantly demonstrate the transformative power of unwavering vision. An oceanographer and explorer, Earle has maintained a consistent vision of ocean conservation throughout her career, leading over 100 expeditions and spending more than 7,000 hours underwater. Her "Hope Spots" initiative—setting aside ecologically unique areas of the ocean designated for protection under a global conservation campaign overseen by another of her organizations, Mission Blue—demonstrates how personal vision and values can evolve into global conservation efforts.

Oxford trained lawyer and management consultant, Roz Savage of the UK appeared to have it all—the job, the house, the relationship, the sports car, etc. Yet, all that success didn't make her happy. Something was missing, and she began some serious soul-searching. One day she sat down to write her own obituary, the epitaph she wanted to have at the end of her life. She thought of obituaries of people that had stuck with her. *Those people were adventurers and risk-takers,* she mused, *people who seemed to have lived many lifetimes in one, people who tried lots of things, some of them successes, some of them spectacular failures. But at least they'd had the guts to try.* Thinking such things, she knew her life had to change. She left her corporate career to "find herself," and after a varied and circuitous route, set about connecting with a cause that mattered to her—the environment. Savage's vision of inspiring environmental awareness through adventure ultimately led her to become the first woman to row solo across the Atlantic, Pacific, and Indian oceans. In her book *Rowing the Atlantic: Lessons Learned on the Open Ocean,* she writes: "I don't for a moment think I am any braver or better than anybody else ... when that thunderbolt of an idea first hit me and inspired me to row across oceans, it filled me with a sense of purpose so strong that it overcame my fears. Even when boredom, frustration, fatigue or despair threatened to overwhelm me, it was that powerful sense of purpose that kept me going."[39]

Her experiences teach us that vision isn't merely about seeing what lies ahead—it's about maintaining that vision through adversity and adaptation. And her latest adventure? In an effort to continue to advance environmental and social policies to create a better world, Roz Savage began serving as an elected Member of Parliament of the UK in 2024.

The art of inspiring leadership

The pioneer of the contemporary field of leadership studies, Warren Bennis once observed that "Leadership is the capacity to translate vision into reality." This translation requires not just the articulation of vision but the ability to inspire others to share and pursue it. The most effective leaders create what Robert Greenleaf called "servant leadership," where the vision serves the highest needs of all stakeholders.

The most effective leaders understand that inspiration flows not from grand speeches or dramatic gestures, but from consistent alignment between words and actions. They inspire through authenticity, demonstrating genuine commitment to shared values and vision. They have presence and are fully engaged and attentive in interactions with team members. They generate hope and empowerment, maintaining and communicating optimism while acknowledging challenges. At the same time, they create opportunities for others to discover and express their potential. And they take action, converting promises into tangible progress.

> *The most effective leaders understand that inspiration flows not from grand speeches or dramatic gestures, but from consistent alignment between words and actions.*

But there is more to leadership that doesn't get talked about much, and that is wonder, inspiration, joy and hope.

Wonder is the foundation. It represents a form of love for existence itself, an openness to being moved and transformed by experience. This is the feeling of awe and amazement at something beautiful, surprising, or inexplicable. It's the sense of openness and curiosity about the world around us. Wonder often arises from experiencing something new, unexpected, or grand, whether it's a natural phenomenon (like a starry night), a work of art, or a human achievement. Wonder creates a fertile ground for the other emotions. When we are filled with wonder, we are more receptive to inspiration, joy, and hope. Wonder can be a powerful source of inspiration. When we are awestruck by something, it can ignite a desire within us to create something equally beautiful or meaningful.

Inspiration is the spark. Inspiration is the feeling of being mentally stimulated to do or create something. It's a surge of enthusiasm and motivation that drives us to pursue a goal or express ourselves. Inspiration often leads to joy as we engage in the creative process and experience the satisfaction of bringing something new into the world.

Joy is the Fuel. Joy is a feeling of great pleasure and happiness. It's a positive emotion that arises from experiencing something good and fulfilling. Joy, in turn, fuels our inspiration, making us more likely to persist in our endeavors and overcome challenges.

Hope is the Sustainer. Hope is a feeling of expectation and desire for a certain thing to happen. It's a belief that a positive outcome is possible, even in the face of seeming insurmountable difficulties. It sustains us through challenging times, giving us the strength to keep going even when we don't want to. As Emily Dickenson once put it: "Hope is the thing with feathers that perches in the soul and sings the tune without words and never stops at all."

When we experience the positive emotions of wonder, inspiration, joy, and hope, we are more likely to believe in the possibility of a better future. Together these four emotions work in a beautiful cycle, enriching our lives and motivating us to pursue our dreams, aspirations, visions, and goals.

Keeping the fire of inspiration burning

Inspiration by its very nature is a temporary thing. Sustaining the positive momentum it triggers in a human being or a nation demands the cultivation of sustainable enthusiasm—a steady flame rather than a brief flash. This cultivation involves curiosity—maintaining genuine interest in learning and discovery. It requires purpose, connecting actions to meaningful goals. And it thrives on reflection, the regular consideration of progress and meaning.

One of the strongest elements in sustaining enthusiasm and maintaining momentum is community. Engaging with others who share similar vision and aspirations, we can practice developing the emotions and outlook that sustain inspiration together. Inspiration, while deeply personal, thrives in community. This understanding appears in many wisdom traditions, from the Confucian emphasis on virtuous friendship to the Christian concept of fellowship, as just two examples. It suggests that inspiration, while internal in nature, flourishes with external nourishment and shared accountability.

Community also aids inspiration by providing active resistance to cynical impulses that often try to pose as wisdom, but are actual threats to progress, beauty, and possibility. Bullies often attempt to employ cynicism and criticism as tools to gain influence and power. Fear and coercion are their weapons of choice. Successful organizations—including churches and clubs—fight cynicism through regular recognition and celebration of achievements, the sharing of inspiring stories and examples, through the cultivation of supportive relationships, and the intentional creation of spaces for wonder and reflection.

Practical applications and benefits

The practical benefits of maintaining clear vision manifest in multiple ways:

> **Resilience:** Vision provides a reference point during challenges, helping maintain direction through adversity. As Viktor Frankl noted from his concentration camp experiences, "Those who have a 'why' to live, can bear with almost any 'how.'"
>
> **Decision-making:** Clear vision simplifies decision-making by providing criteria against which to evaluate options. Austrian American management consultant, and author Peter Drucker's question, "Does this decision advance our vision?" becomes a powerful tool for strategic choice.
>
> **Motivation:** Vision creates what psychologists call "pull motivation"—drawing us forward rather than pushing from behind. This intrinsic motivation proves more sustainable than external incentives.
>
> **Alignment:** Shared vision enables coordination without constant supervision, what management

theorist Mary Parker Follett called "power with" rather than "power over."

Conclusion

The cultivation of inspiration and vision requires intentional practice. Key steps include:

- Regular exposure to inspiring ideas, people and places (Turn off the news and take a walk in nature.)
- Creation of space for reflection and wonder (Step away from that screen.)
- Development of gratitude practices (Before you sleep, ask, "What's one thing I am grateful for today?")
- Engagement in challenging but meaningful pursuits (I can do this hard thing in order to learn something that matters to me.)
- Cultivation of supportive relationships (Check yourself here. Do you allow yourself to be supported? Do you support others?)
- Regular celebration of progress and achievement (This is a good self-kindness practice. It's not bragging! Consider it nourishment for the soul.)

Inspiration isn't a destination but a continuous journey of growth and discovery. It requires vision and a regular renewal of both growth and discovery through conscious practice and community support. By understanding inspiration as a force that can be cultivated and shared, we enhance our capacity for meaningful achievement and joyful perseverance.

Adventure Mindset

Reflective questions

1. What inspires you? Describe a time when you felt deeply inspired. What elements came together to create that experience? How might you intentionally recreate similar conditions?
2. In your current endeavors, how could you better inspire others through your actions and approach? What small (or large) adjustments could make a significant difference?
3. Do you celebrate progress and success in your work or life? What's the criteria to "make the celebration cut?" Do some of your efforts or actions get overlooked using that criterion?
4. Name a few ways you could incorporate celebration to nurture inspiration in yourself and others.
5. Are there aspects of your current professional or personal life that drain your sense of inspiration? How might you transform these elements or shift your relationship to them?

PRINCIPLE #12

PURPOSE AND MEANINGFUL SERVICE

The secret of success is constancy to purpose.

~ Benjamin Disraeli

Many years ago, when I was a student at the University of Oregon, I had the great fortune to meet Buckminster Fuller when he came to Eugene to give a series of talks. An amazingly vibrant 80-year-old, he expressed ideas that were not common at that time—such as his famous declaration, "*You do not belong to you, you belong to the universe*" reflecting his perspective of human existence—that our individual lives are part of a larger, interconnected system.

I'd seen the beautiful geodesic dome he designed for the USA pavilion at 'Expo 67' in Montreal, Canada, about a decade earlier, and was fascinated. Nicknamed "Bucky's Bubble," it was an incredible freestanding building that enclosed an enormous amount of space with minimal structural components. I remember marveling at his energy on the stage as he presented to a large group of students for about 90 minutes and then answered questions for another two hours. During one of his talks, Bucky told a story about going through a critical moment of personal crisis. He had been distraught over business and personal failures. His first child with his wife Anne had died a few years earlier and their second child had just been born. Without an income, with no vision of a positive future, he stood on the shore of Lake Michigan imagining that he would commit suicide by swimming the lake to complete exhaustion and drown. This, he reasoned, would at least give his wife and new baby the life insurance money to make a life going forward. But in that moment, poised between life and death, he heard a voice speaking directly to him: *"You have no right to eliminate yourself,"* the voice said. *"You do not belong to you, you belong to the universe."* Ultimately, instead of killing himself, he decided to see what he could do for the greater good of humanity and nature. A new purpose with a vision for bettering humanity rose in him. He told us he figured if he wasn't successful in this endeavor, that nature would see to his demise, so either way his problem was solved.

At the time I heard Bucky's talk, he called it his "50-year experiment," and viewed it as a "research and development initiative for the planet." This perspective transformed his work in design, architecture, and systems thinking, leading to groundbreaking innovations like the geodesic dome and other significant contributions to sustainable design. "During that half century of time I never wanted for food, clothing, housing, or anything else," he said. "So, I guess fundamentally reorienting my life's purpose worked out."

A way of life

At its core, serving a purpose transcends mere activity—it is a profound commitment to contributing something meaningful to the world. The timeless wisdom captured in the quote, "He profits most who serves best." encapsulates this fundamental truth. Attributed to Arthur Frederick Sheldon, a prominent Rotarian and American business philosopher from the early 20th century, this statement emphasizes that true success is not measured by personal gain, but by the value one creates for others. It's a philosophy that is not about self-diminishment but about recognizing our interconnectedness and the power of collective well-being.

> *Serving a purpose transcends mere activity — it is a profound commitment to contributing something meaningful to the world.*

My father was a Rotarian and the Rotary motto "Service above Self" hung on the wall of his office. A man who served his country during World War II as part of a ground reconnaissance unit in the US Third Army under Gen. George Patton, he was part of the effort to render support and rescue to the encircled troops during the Battle of the Bulge, the last major German offensive campaign on the Western Front during the war. Back at home, for the rest of his life he was active in community service through Rotary and other organizations, giving generously of his time. I grew up being encouraged to find ways to be useful or helpful in some ways to others. At its essence, in my family, helping others was seen as a form of showing love ... love in action as it were.

In my travels, I learned that service is a central theme across diverse spiritual and philosophical traditions. In addition to the Christianity viewpoint, I learned that Hinduism teaches *seva* (selfless service) as a spiritual practice that transcends individual ego. Buddhism views *dana* (selfless giving) as a path to enlightenment and liberation from suffering. Experiencing the world, I learned what a universal view this is, including indigenous wisdom traditions that emphasize community well-being and reciprocal relationships with nature that contribute to something larger than ourselves.

A psychological key to happiness

Having a worthwile purpose that is larger than oneself, serving some greater good, is an important key to a meaningful and fulfilling life. Frankly, the happiest and most fulfilled people I've ever seen have been those who are in service to others or to some greater good beyond them.

Research in positive psychology consistently demonstrates that individuals who engage in meaningful service, experience an increased sense of personal fulfillment, enhanced self-worth and personal significance, reduced feelings of isolation, increased social connection, improved mental health and emotional resilience, and a broader perspective on life's challenges and opportunities.

Leadership and love in action

By helping others, we translate abstract emotional connections into tangible actions. This "love in action" creates a reciprocal cycle of compassion and understanding that enriches both the giver and the receiver. In the realms of leadership, the concept of servant leadership challenges traditional hierarchical models. Coined by the American pioneer of humanist business philosophy Robert K. Greenleaf in 1970, this approach prioritizes the growth, well-being, and empowerment of team members and communities over personal power or status.[40] It represents a sophisticated approach to leadership that recognizes true power lies in lifting others, creating environments of trust, and enabling collective potential—a principle long understood by successful expedition leaders and adventurers whose ability to inspire and guide is rooted in their commitment to serving their team's needs and shared objectives. In challenging situations like polar expeditions, humanitarian missions, and environmental movements, service becomes not just an ideal but a survival strategy.

Granted, most service is not conducted under extreme circumstances. But no matter the conditions, what counts in the realm of service is, as former US President Jimmy Carter once put it, that it be conducted "in a way that neither exalts ourselves nor is demeaning to the recipients."

Bottomline, by shifting our perspective from self-centeredness to interconnected service, we unlock profound opportunities for growth, happiness, and meaningful contribution. As we navigate the complexities of modern life, the timeless wisdom remains clear: Our greatest fulfillment comes not from what we accumulate, but from what we contribute. In serving others, we ultimately serve ourselves, creating a virtuous cycle of growth, understanding, and shared humanity.

Reflective questions

1. If you were to look back on your life 20 or 30 years from now, what meaningful contributions would you hope to have made?
2. How might reframing your current goals through the lens of service change your approach to them?
3. Is there a cause or issue that deeply moves you or makes you feel passionate about creating change?
4. If you could dedicate one year of your life to making a significant difference, what would you choose to focus on? Why?
5. Reflect on a time when serving others unexpectedly transformed something in you—your perspective or even your life. What changed for you? What did you learn?
6. How might developing a more service-oriented mindset contribute to your personal growth and emotional resilience?

PRINCIPLE #13

RESPONSIBILITY AND ACCOUNTABILITY: THE FOUNDATION OF HUMAN POTENTIAL

*Until the great mass of the people shall be filled with
the sense of responsibility for each other's welfare,
social justice can never be attained.*

~ Helen Keller

In the vast tapestry of human experience, few qualities are as fundamental to personal growth and societal harmony as responsibility and accountability. These interconnected virtues form the bedrock of individual integrity, social trust, and collective progress.

At its core, responsibility is a conscious choice to acknowledge our role in shaping outcomes, to recognize the ripple effects of our words and actions, and to stand firmly in the center of our own life's narrative. It's not about accepting blame, but rather about embracing our ability to respond to life's circumstances; to choose, to act, and to create

> **Responsibility is a conscious choice to acknowledge our role in shaping outcomes, to recognize the ripple effects of our words and actions, and to stand firmly in the center of our own life's narrative.**

meaningful change. In other words, our *response-ability*.

In Judaism, the concept of Tikkun (or Tikkun Olam) is rooted in both rabbinic literature and mystical traditions, and often interpreted as "repairing the world", encompassing actions aimed at improving the world, including the environment, society, and addressing social justice issues. In Stoic philosophy, personal responsibility is viewed as the ultimate expression of human freedom. Returning to the quote by Marcus Aurelius, "You have power over your mind, not outside events. Realize this, and you will find strength"—this profound insight suggests that responsibility begins with mastering one's internal responses, regardless of external circumstances. In the Buddhist view, responsibility means being able to respond to life's challenges with awareness and courage, transforming responsibility from a burden into an opportunity for profound personal transformation. "It is the fundamental ground of human dignity," said Tibetan Buddhist teacher Chögyam Trungpa Rinpoche.

Indigenous wisdom traditions often frame responsibility as a spiritual covenant with the natural world. Native American elder Luther Standing Bear of the Lakota tribe articulated this beautifully: "Man's heart away from nature becomes hard; the Creator's lessons are written in every flower, leaf, and rock." Here, responsibility extends beyond human interactions to include our relationship with the entire web of life.

The ancient Hawaiian perspective

But it is within the ancient Hawaiian culture that responsibility, viewed as it is through the lens of interconnectedness, exhibits the greatest possible depth and meaning. As I write this, I'm on the island of Kauai, sitting near where the Wailua River joins the ocean. There are many signs of the ancient Hawaiian ancestors here—nearby petroglyphs and heiau formations—sacred ceremonial sites built of lava rock long before the Europeans arrived. A place blessed with much natural beauty and an abundance of resources to support and inspire the healthy growth of a healthy population, it's easy to see why the ancient leaders of their society made this area the main center of governance on Kauai all those many centuries ago. Governance heavily grounded in personal responsibility or "kuliana."

Unlike the English word responsibility, "kuliana" encompasses a more holistic concept embracing personal integrity, commitment to community, spiritual accountability, and a wholehearted engagement with one's roles and relationships. It also lays the philosophical groundwork for one of the most unique approaches to personal responsibility in the world: The powerful healing practice of Ho'oponopono (*pronounced* hō-ō-pōnō-pōnō*)*.

Unlike the Western concept of responsibility that is purely individual and often focused on blame or punishment, Ho'oponopono is a process of forgiveness, reconciliation, self-healing, and collective harmony based on the revolutionary—but scientifically established—fact that we are fundamentally connected with everyone and everything around us. Because of this interconnection (which Eastern mystics call "Oneness"), we are responsible for everything and everyone that shows up in our experience. Here's a story that demonstrates what I mean. Hawaiian therapist Dr. Ihaleakala Hew Len worked at the Hawaii State Hospital of mental health services in Kaneohe, Oahu, Hawai'i between 1984-1987. A firm believer in the power of Ho'oponopono, he applied the healing forgiveness practice, which I will describe shortly, to all the patients he was assigned. Which means as he read each patient's chart, various thoughts, judgments, and emotions would come up—upset, rage, embarrassment, pity, disgust, you name it. And as he was reading and experiencing these reactions in himself, he took responsibility for those thoughts, judgments and emotions as his own projections based on his perceptions of the patient, what he was reading, and what he knew of them personally. And every day he forgave the patient and himself for all the negative things he perceived—what he called "cleaning up" the projections in the quantum field. And as he did this practice, the patients on the ward started getting better, until one by one they were released back into society. After four years the ward was closed, and he was out of a job. He deemed this as success.

Unbelievable? Not to Dr. Len who wrote about this experience with American singer-songwriter and author Joe Vitale in their book *Zero Limits*.[41] By his own admission he did no other "therapy" with any of those patients, just Ho'oponopono, a healing approach as simple as it is apparently potent. The traditional Ho'oponopono prayer / practice involves just four key phrases which are either spoken aloud or mentally chanted when every limiting thought, judgment, and emotional reaction occurs:

- "I'm sorry. Please forgive me. Thank you. I love you."

So, what's actually happening during this process? According to Dr. Len and other practitioners of Ho'oponopono, these simple words and the intention behind them represent a profound "reset" in the universal quantum field and in the mental, emotional, physical, and spiritual energy fields of the individuals involved by:

- Taking responsibility for one's thoughts and energy
- Releasing negative patterns and energies
- Seeking forgiveness from both self and others for those negative energies
- Expressing gratitude for the healing
- Cultivating unconditional love

And before you dismiss this altogether, please realize the approach Ho'oponopono takes toward healing is strongly aligned with speculation on how Jesus performed his healing miracles: By dismissing any negative thoughts of disease and then, *through consciousness alone,* realigning the quantum field and the energy fields of the sick person to match the new reality.

At the very least modern psychological research validates what wisdom traditions still understand, namely that taking responsibility is crucial for mental health, personal growth, and social functioning. When individuals embrace responsibility, they experience:

- Enhanced Self-Esteem: By owning their actions, people develop a stronger sense of personal agency and competence.

- Improved Relationships: Accountability builds trust, fostering deeper and more authentic connections with others.

- Reduced Stress: Paradoxically, taking responsibility reduces psychological burden by eliminating victim mentality and uncertainty.

- Accelerated Learning: Recognizing and learning from mistakes becomes a pathway to continuous personal development.

Conversely, avoiding responsibility comes with significant personal and societal costs. Lying, deflecting blame, and refusing to acknowledge one's role in outcomes create a cascade of negative consequences, including erosion of trust in relationships, stunted personal growth and increased psychological stress. Maintaining facades and avoiding responsibility is inherently exhausting!

Accountability

The word *accountable,* on the other hand, originates from the Latin word *computare,* which means "to count." In this sense, to be accountable means that a person responsible for nature or other people or money and other assets has to be able to produce "a count" regarding that which has been left in their care. *Accountability* is the ability to produce tangible proof of having lived up to one's responsibilities.

Responsibility and Accountability: The Foundation of Human Potential

Across diverse cultures, the concept of accountability emerges as a fundamental social and spiritual principle. In Japanese culture, the concept of "Sekinin" extends beyond mere legal or professional responsibility. It encompasses a holistic sense of moral obligation, where one's actions reflect not just on themselves, but on their family, organization, and broader social network. This perspective sees accountability as a sacred trust, a living connection between individual choices and collective well-being. In Hinduism, the concept of "karma" represents a universal law of cause and effect, where every action or inaction generates consequences that shape one's future experiences. In other words, if you can't be accountable to what you are responsible for, you pay for it. There is no escaping accountability. At most, it can be delayed. Sometimes, the longer it is delayed, the "amount due" may come with compound interest.

> **There is no escaping accountability. At most, it can be delayed. Sometimes, the longer it is delayed, the "amount due" may come with compound interest.**

American businessperson and philanthropist William Clement Stone started off hawking newspapers in restaurants in 1905 as a very young child. Over the course of his life he rose in the business ranks to eventually become a multimillionaire. Famous for his polka-dot bow ties, pencil-thin moustache, and his firm belief in accountability and action as the foundation of success, Stone advised "Take 100 percent responsibility for your life, and everything you do, and everything that does or does not happen to you."[42]

When we are grounded in the reality that we are 100 percent responsible, accountability comes naturally, finding ways to take action to protect and nourish what we are responsible for. When we take full ownership of our lives, the circumstances we face, and the results we get, we can more effectively lead ourselves and others toward solutions and changes until we get the outcomes we want.

Hawaiian accountability

In our fragmented, individualistic modern world, Hawaiian approaches to responsibility offer a powerful alternative. Responsibility and accountability go hand-in-hand. They remind us that accountability is not about guilt or control, but about taking strong positive action to create healing, connection, and mutual transformation. In practice, traditional Hawaiianss approach accountability in several ways:

- Community decision-making that prioritizes collective well-being
- Deep respect for elders and ancestral wisdom
- Application of Ho'oponopono to heal divisions and conflicts
- Environmental stewardship as a spiritual and practical responsibility
- Conflict resolution focused on healing rather than punishment
- Personal growth seen as a collective journey

Ho'oponopono, in particular, has gained international recognition as a powerful personal development and healing technique. Its core message is revolutionary: True change begins within us, and by taking complete responsibility for our inner state, we can positively influence our reality.

The Hawaiians perspective invites us to see responsibility and accountability not as a burden, but as a sacred opportunity for personal and collective healing. It suggests that by embracing our interconnectedness and approaching life with love, integrity, and conscious awareness, we can transform not just ourselves, but the world around us.

Reflective questions
Ask yourself:

1. **Self-awareness inquiry:** When was the last time I truly took full responsibility for a mistake or challenge, without making excuses or blaming external circumstances? How did that effect the situation? What did I learn about myself in that moment, and how did it change my approach to future challenges?

2. **Relationship dynamics:** How do my current patterns of responsibility and accountability impact my closest relationships? Are there ways I could be more transparent, honest, and fully present in my commitments to others?

3. **Team and organizational impact:** In the teams or organizations I'm part of, how does a culture of accountability (or lack thereof) influence overall performance, trust, and collective achievement? What role can I play in fostering a more accountable

environment? (Hint: Waiting for someone else to do it may not be your best option.)

4. **Systemic reflection:** Beyond individual actions, how do I contribute to or challenge systemic patterns of avoiding responsibility in my community, workplace, or broader social circles?

PRINCIPLE # 14

STRATEGIC PATIENCE

Patience is bitter, but its fruit is sweet.

~ Jean-Jacques Rousseau

A mentor of mine many years ago would sometimes say, "Speed can waste time." And I discovered the truth of this the hard way many times. But one of the most memorable lessons came back in the days when I rode freight trains. Hitching free rides around the country, I would spend long hours in and around freight yards waiting for trains. Unlike passenger trains or airplanes, etc., there were no published schedules, at least none I had access to, so waiting was part of the deal. Also, unlike public passenger trains and airplanes, the "waiting area" was noisy and noxious with fumes and spilled debris that was often toxic. The yards had no shelter and rarely any shade.

I read a lot of books as I waited for freight trains. But there was one time I didn't wait long enough. It was December and the rail yard in Eugene, Oregon was drizzly and cold. I was eager to get south to Arizona where there was

Adventure Mindset

sunshine and warmth waiting for me. And in my impatience, I jumped on the wrong train. Although it started going in the right direction, it later took a turn I'd not planned for. I thought it was headed south all the way from Eugene to Los Angeles, but the Southern Pacific train I got on turned east near Susanville and headed over the Sierra Nevada range, going east across northern Nevada, with an ultimate destination of Chicago.

Now, the average temperatures in many areas of the Cascade and Sierra Nevada mountains in December are below freezing. It was a cold ride traveling on a freight train through those mountains and across northern Nevada as the train lumbered toward my first opportunity to get off in Ogden, Utah. From there I eventually made my way south and then back west to Los Angeles and then east to Arizona. It was an incredibly long detour that exposed me to more danger than I'd planned for. So, you can imagine, I never forgot the value of patience again after that. It's forever etched in my memory!

Strategic patience

As humans, we are naturally wired for immediate gratification. Our evolutionary history prioritized quick decisions that ensured survival—react quickly or perish. However, as the above story shows, in our complex modern world, this instinctual response often leads to suboptimal (and subzero) outcomes.

A powerful method of engaging with complexity, strategic patience is the deliberate choice to observe, prepare, and act with precision rather than succumbing to impulses and thoughtless reactions. At its core, this approach recognizes that true progress is not always linear, and that meaningful transformation requires a delicate balance between forward momentum and thoughtful recalibration.

While seemingly modern, strategic patience, however, is nothing new. Many indigenous cultures view time and progress as cyclical rather than linear. The Native American concept of "waiting for the medicine" suggests that healing and transformation cannot be rushed. As well, the ancient Chinese philosophical concept of "wu-wei" offers profound insights into strategic patience. Often translated as "non-action" or "effortless action," wu-wei describes action that is in harmony with the natural flow of circumstances. As the 6th century BC Chinese philosopher Lao Tzu wrote in the *Tao Te Ching*: "Do you have the patience to wait until your mud settles and the water is clear? Can you remain unmoving until the right action arises by itself?"[43]

This suggests that true mastery involves understanding when to act and when to allow situations to unfold naturally. It's not about forceful intervention, but represents a sophisticated understanding of natural flow and the ability to sense the optimal timing for engagement. In Taoist philosophy, wu-wei is often compared to the behavior of water—yielding yet persistent, flowing around obstacles rather than confronting them directly. Water doesn't struggle, yet ultimately prevails. Over time, it can wear down even the hardest stone.

At its core, wu-wei is about aligning oneself with the Tao (道), the fundamental nature of the universe. It suggests that there is an intrinsic order and rhythm to life, and that true mastery comes from recognizing and harmonizing with

> *There is an intrinsic order and rhythm to life, and true mastery comes from recognizing and harmonizing with this natural flow*

this natural flow rather than attempting to forcefully impose one's will upon it.

While often perceived as exclusively Eastern, modern complexity theory and systems thinking have begun to validate many of wu-wei's fundamental insights. These fields demonstrate that complex systems often self-organize most effectively when given space and minimal intervention. Wu-wei also shares fascinating parallels with Western philosophical and psychological concepts:

- **Stoic Acceptance:** The Stoic principle of focusing on what one can control
- **Jungian Synchronicity:** The idea of meaningful coincidences emerging when one is in flow
- **Systems Thinking:** Understanding complex adaptive systems and their inherent self-organizing principles

Masters of strategic patience

Unsurprisingly, throughout history, the most successful explorers tend to be the most patient strategic planners. Unlike British Royal Navy officer and explorer Robert Falcon Scott, who perished along with five companions on an expedition to the South Pole in 1912, Norwegian explorer Roald Amundsen's successful South Pole expedition in 1911 was a remarkable example of strategic patience and planning.

Amundsen's approach wasn't about rushing to get the job done, but about creating a sustainable, well-planned expedition. He spent years meticulously preparing, studying indigenous Arctic cultures, learning survival techniques from the Inuit people, carefully selecting and training his team in these techniques—an approach that perhaps could have spelled the survival of Scott and his team, who died on the ice just 12.5 miles from the next available supply depot.[44]

Oceanographer Robert Ballard's discovery of the wreck of the Titanic in 1987 wasn't a sudden achievement, but the result of years of persistent research, careful planning, and technological development. Unlike all failed attempts to locate the ship before him, Ballard recognized that the depth at which the Titanic rested (12,500 feet) and the vast seabed area to be searched due to the inaccuracies in the early estimations of the Titanic's location would require a completely different search approach. He and his team spent decades at the Woods Hole Oceanographic Institution developing a remotely operated vehicle (ROV) called the Argo, as well as a side-scan sonar system, to conduct a methodical search of the ocean floor. Their patience paid off when they discovered the wreckage of the Titanic lying on the seabed on September 1, 1987.[45]

In my mountain climbing experiences, I've seen time and again how impatience costs lives and how patience pays dividends. The often-repeated adage of "Getting to the top is optional. Getting down is mandatory," encapsulates this well. Recognizing when environmental conditions, personal fitness, or team dynamics suggest halting progress is not failure—it's wisdom.

Sometimes simply waiting for the weather to change when you're out for a casual hike can be life changing. I remember one time when my wife and I were hiking along a high ridgeline as a thunderstorm looked to be building. Thunder booming in the distance, we wondered if this was really a *storm* or just a small *squall* that we could navigate. We reached a shallow rock overhang that could provide a bit of shelter from the rain, if indeed it did arrive, and decided to pause rather than push on.

We'd been there for less than a minute when a lightning strike hit on the trail right in front of us. We were close enough to see the dust kicked up where the lightning bolt hit the rocks. If we'd stayed on pace and not paused when and where we did, it's likely that one or both of us might not be alive today. Sometimes strategic patience happens when you don't even know it's strategic. The other element I see at work here *is Jungian Synchronicity*—the idea of meaningful coincidences emerging when one is in flow.[46] Indeed.

Balancing patience with decisive action—the "wu-wei" approach to living—can be developed and strengthened to feel more natural to you. Try the following:

- **Slow down** to notice where you are, what you are doing, and where your attention is.
- **Build capacity** during down times: Strengthen resources, oneself, and others.
- **Mindfulness meditation:** Develop the capacity to observe without immediate reaction.
- **Regular self-reflection:** Am I present, right here, right now? Or am I in next week's or last week's meeting? Am I really in conversation with a person or

is my strategy to be in my head with my thoughts and opinions, waiting for my turn to opine, or waiting for it to be over? You can adjust your strategy. Perhaps be strategically patient in order to experience something unexpected or learn a piece of the "story" that changes the course of a decision path, or, or, or ... you get the picture.

- **Use stress management techniques** to build emotional resilience: Breathing practices, body scanning practice, letting go practice.
- **Scenario planning:** Mentally rehearse multiple potential outcomes before acting.
- **Continuous learning:** Stay adaptable and informed. See obstacles as learning.

Modern benefits and applications

In a world that often celebrates forceful action and constant intervention, strategic patience offers the profound alternative of transformation through understanding, influence through alignment, and power through sensitivity to natural rhythms.

Modern neuroscience provides fascinating insights into the benefits of strategic patience. For example, practicing patience activates the prefrontal cortex associated with executive functions like planning, decision-making, and emotional regulation. This neurological engagement helps us to reduce stress by avoiding reactive behaviors, improve emotional intelligence enabling us to make more considered, comprehensive decisions, as well as develop greater resilience and adaptability.

> **The journey of strategic patience is ultimately a journey of self-mastery**

The journey of strategic patience is ultimately a journey of self-mastery—a continuous practice of balancing action and reflection, movement and stillness, ambition and acceptance. The number of arenas in which this practice can prove to be an advantage are almost too numerous to count, including:

- **Psychological flexibility**: Developing the capacity to respond rather than react.

- **Personal development**: Rather than forcefully changing oneself, wu-wei proposes creating conditions where natural growth and transformation can occur.

- **Ecological wisdom:** The lens of wu-wei reveals that forcing systems often creates more resistance and complications. (We see this in organizational systems).

- **Conflict resolution:** Interpersonal conflicts in business and personal relationships can be more easily resolved via finding solutions that allow all parties to feel their fundamental needs are met, rather than enabling the old game of winners and losers.

- **Organizational dynamics**: Leaders practicing wu-wei create environments of psychological safety, trust, and intrinsic motivation, where team members can self-organize and innovate.

- **Leadership:** Understanding that true leadership comes from alignment rather than control is a game changer.

In a world that constantly demands immediate responses, those who master strategic patience gain a profound competitive advantage. They become not just survivors, but true navigators of complexity, able to read subtle signals, conserve energy, and strike with precision when the moment is right.

Reflective questions

Remember, strategic patience is about cultivating a dynamic awareness that allows for more intelligent, nuanced responses to life's challenges. The following questions may help in that discovery.

1. **Moment of pause**: Recall a recent situation where you rushed a decision. What might have been different if you had taken more time to observe, reflect, and carefully consider your options? What insights can you gain from imagining a more patient approach?

2. **Personal growth landscape**: Where are you most patient? Where are you least patient? Think about a significant personal shift you've experienced or are currently navigating. How has patience played a role in your journey? Where have you struggled with impatience, and what might you learn from embracing a more strategic, longer-term perspective?

3. **Organizational learning**: Consider an organization or system you're familiar with. Where do you observe a lack of strategic patience creating inefficiencies or missed opportunities? What might a more patient approach look like in terms of innovation, problem-solving, or change management?

4. **Embodied awareness**: We can learn to "catch ourself" early allowing us to consider our options before reacting. Our body gives us feelings and emotional feedback, so listen for it and decide what the message is. Use your body scanning practice to assess what your brain may be ignoring.

5. What other physical and emotional practices might help you develop greater capacity for patient, intentional engagement with life's complexities?

PRINCIPLE #15

GRATITUDE AND THE ALCHEMY OF APPRECIATION AND WONDER

Gratitude is the healthiest of all human emotions. The more you express gratitude for what you have, the more likely you will have even more to express gratitude for.

~ Zig Ziglar

Freighthopping in my youth apparently taught me more than I realized. Not only did it teach me the value of strategic patience, it taught me gratitude. As you know from my previous story, I had learned (almost to my demise), that the windchill factor on a moving train can drop to dangerous levels especially if riding in the open air. Even if dressed warmly, the cold can be life-threatening crossing higher elevations if one is not prepared and lucky.

Although I was dressed for winter weather and had a warm sleeping bag with me, with colder winter temperatures setting in, I was hoping to avoid a flatcar for the early, coldest parts of that journey. Railroad companies were beginning to phase out boxcars because they are less efficient to load and unload than flatcars, so it was getting harder to find an empty boxcar to ride in.

As it happened, I was able to find a relatively clean empty boxcar to settle into, and I remember nearly bursting with joy for my tremendous, good fortune. I'll never forget riding through that winter wonderland with glistening fresh snow blanketing towering evergreen trees, watching some of the most beautiful scenery in the world pass by as I snuggled warmly in my sleeping bag, safely held within the walls of that boxcar.

Granted, it could be observed that a "relatively clean" boxcar is not really clean, except in comparison to the ones that aren't. And when they are empty and don't ride on the tracks as smoothly as when they are full, they tend to bounce and vibrate a lot. And the ride is very noisy—basically the opposite of luxury. And yet, considering the possible alternatives, my gratitude was well deserved and very real. One of the results of looking at life through the lens of adventure is realizing that life can be beautiful, amazing, and hard—all at the same time!

The essence of gratitude

Far from being a passive emotion, gratitude is an active, dynamic way of engaging with life that has the potential to reshape our inner landscape and our external experiences. At its core, gratitude is the recognition of goodness that exists beyond ourselves. It's the ability to see and appreciate the gifts, large and small, that continuously flow into our lives—gifts that all too often go unnoticed and unacknowledged. Which is one of the reasons being an adventurer—or simply developing the adventure mindset—ends up being so satisfying. Gifts, large and small, are constantly getting placed in your path. You're hiking in the rainforest at dusk, your footfalls silent on a trail with thousands of years of moss built up underfoot. You round a bend just in time to see a full-grown male mountain lion leap into the path not ten feet in front of you. Mutually surprised, you both stop and stare at each other in wonder. You're so close you can see where the beige fur on the lion's muzzle turns black where his whiskers enter. His huge golden eyes blink. And then he bounds off the trail and into the forest, leaving you dizzy with gratitude for his swift departure yet filled with wonder and gratitude that he was ever there in the first place.

> **Developing the adventure mindset, gifts, large and small are constantly getting placed in your path.**

Or you're sleeping on top of a butte in South Dakota with no tent, and you wake up in the middle of the night because your air mattress developed a leak and all the air seeped out and now you're lying on the rocks, mentally grumbling about having to get up in the cold night air to find the pump in your backpack. And suddenly coyotes start yipping on other plateaus around you, and, as they do, an iridescent curtain of purple and green ripples across the heavens above you. It's like the sky itself is moving. And for hours you lie there, cold ground and rocks forgotten, watching as the Northen Lights turn your world into an extravaganza of nighttime color.

Many hikers and others who spend time outdoors report that extended time in nature cultivates a deep sense of gratitude. When we are immersed in the world of nature, it demands presence in order for us to stay safe. And it opens our hearts to want to keep nature safe as well. With each step, intentional "seeing" creates an intimacy. We see beauty and devastation. We see the habitat of multitudes of animals and insects all playing their part in the natural web of life. Our "noticing" skill sharpens and widens. Our appreciation knows no bounds. We don't want to miss *anything*.

Pacific Crest and Appalachian Trail journals are filled with accounts of hikers talking about how they're shocked to be appreciating the simple things in life—water, rest, and human connection—in ways they never had before. "Gratitude turns whatever I have into enough, and more," said renowned explorer and writer Alastair Humphreys. "It transforms ordinary days into adventures and ordinary opportunities into blessings."[47] Jessica Watson, an Australian sailor who was awarded the Order of Australia Medal after conducting a solo circumnavigation of the Earth at the age of 16, spoke luminously about finding joy and resilience through appreciating the smallest positive experiences on that voyage.[48]

In such ways, gratitude and wonder are intimately connected, forming a powerful duo that can transform our perception of reality. Wonder invites us to see the extraordinary in the ordinary, while gratitude allows us to deeply appreciate these moments of marvel. Which is, no doubt, why so many religious and spiritual systems see gratitude as a spiritual practice.

In Hinduism, "prasad" is the practice of receiving blessings or food as a divine gift, recognizing that abundance comes from a source greater than ourselves. The Bible speaks of gratitude as the way our spirits deepen our connection with God. In Buddhist philosophy, gratitude is seen as a form of meditation—a practice of mindful appreciation. The concept of "mudita" (sympathetic joy) encourages practitioners to find joy in the happiness of others, expanding gratitude beyond personal experience. If nothing else, it puts things in their proper perspective. As one traditional Buddhist teaching puts it: "Let us rise up and be thankful, for if we didn't learn a lot today, at least we learned a little, and if we didn't learn a little, at least we didn't get sick, and if we got sick, at least we didn't die; so, let us all be thankful."

> *"Let us rise up and be thankful, for if we didn't learn a lot today, at least we learned a little, and if we didn't learn a little, at least we didn't get sick, and if we got sick, at least we didn't die; so, let us all be thankful."*

The opposite of paranoia

Neurological research has revealed fascinating insights into the power of gratitude. For example, practicing gratitude increases dopamine and serotonin levels and has an effect similar to antidepressants. Regular gratitude practices can literally rewire neural pathways, making positive thinking more natural. And grateful individuals consistently demonstrate lower stress levels and improved overall mental health.

Which brings me to the interesting psychological state known as pronoia. A neologism that may have been originally coined in 1982 by American astrologer, author and musician Rob Brezsny, pronoia is the exact opposite of paranoia, and characterized by feeling that the world is conspiring on your behalf rather than against you. In his book, *Pronoia Is the Antidote for Paranoia*, Brezsny teaches readers to reimagine the world as a compassionate miracle, inviting them into a radical trust in life's fundamental goodness.[49] Gratitude is an essential tool with which they reframe their worldview from a negative reactive emotion to a proactive stance of anticipatory appreciation.

In his book, *The 7 Habits of Highly Effective People*, American businessman and educator, Stephen Covey, taught that there are enough resources and opportunities on the planet for everyone.[50] Developing gratitude was one of the methods by which people could create an abundance mindset, all the while consciously reducing competitive thinking, encouraging collaboration, and celebrating others' successes. Seeing opportunities everywhere and being grateful for them, Covey said, was the key to success.

Gratitude Practices

- **Awareness:** Consciously recognize and acknowledge the positive elements in life when they show up.
- **Appreciation:** Reflect on positive experiences. What made them special for you?

- **Expression:** Acknowledge and share your gratitude with others—often.
- **Giving back:** Create a pay-it-forward habit. Understand your interconnectedness with the world and realize "What goes out must come back."
- **Gratitude journaling:** Capture three to five things you're grateful for daily. Write them or speak them into a digital journal recording.
- **Gratitude letters:** Write heartfelt notes of thanks to people who have impacted your life.
- **Mindful acceptance:** Pause throughout the day to recognize small moments of grace when they arrive.

Conclusion

Gratitude is not about forcing positivity or denying life's challenges. Instead, it is a courageous act of seeing beauty, recognizing interconnectedness, and choosing to focus on what enriches our experience. In a world that so often emphasizes what is wrong, gratitude becomes a revolutionary act. An invitation to see differently, to feel deeply, and to allow for and recognize the continuous flow of goodness, grace, and good fortune that surrounds us.

Reflective questions

Pick one (or two if you are feeling ambitious) and take a moment to know yourself better by asking yourself:

1. When was a moment in my life when I felt profound gratitude that went beyond simple thanks—a

moment of deep appreciation that seemed to shift my entire perception of reality? What made that experience so transformative, and how did it change my understanding of myself and the world?

2. Reflecting on the people, experiences, or circumstances that I often take for granted, what would my life look like if I truly recognized and appreciated these "invisible" sources of support, comfort, and opportunity? How might my daily experience change if I approached these elements with genuine thankfulness?

3. Considering a challenging or painful experience in my life, can I identify any unexpected gifts, lessons, or growth that emerged from this difficulty? How might reframing this experience through a lens of gratitude offer a different perspective on resilience and personal transformation?

4. If I were to design a daily practice of gratitude that feels authentic and meaningful to me, what would it look like? What barriers or resistance do I notice within myself when I consider making gratitude a more intentional part of my life?

5. Imagine writing a gratitude letter to an aspect of life you rarely acknowledge—perhaps your body, a particular season, a skill you've developed, or an intangible quality like curiosity or patience. What would you say? What might you discover about yourself in the process of deeply appreciating something you typically overlook?

PRINCIPLE # 16

RECIPROCITY AND GENEROSITY: THE FOUNDATIONS FOR THRIVING

No one has ever become poor by giving.

~ Anne Frank

There are so many stories of generosity in my memory banks, I literally can't choose just one. Perhaps it is the nature of adventure itself, marked as it is with uncertainty and potential peril, that makes those who go on adventures so blessedly generous with each other. Or maybe it's because we spend so much time in nature, the very wellspring of generosity herself, and her abundance rubs off on us. But never have I seen a camper, a hiker, a climber, a kayaker, a biker ... anybody who was in need "out there," not receive a helping hand from one of their fellow travelers on the adventure road.

Even competing in a race or summiting, trying to "get there first," should danger or misfortune befall a fellow competitor on the journey—lost supplies, food washed downstream, a fall, entrapment, someone needing medical attention—if help is anywhere near close, it's offered without a second thought. Like the legendary Sherpas of the Himalayas who share their knowledge, resources, and support with visiting climbers while maintaining deep respect for the mountains, generosity and reciprocity are an accepted part of the game. The part that, most certainly, makes for more meaningful and successful lives all around.

Culturally, perhaps the potlatch ceremonies of the Pacific Northwest Native American tribes exemplify institutionalized generosity and reciprocity best. These elaborate gift-giving festivals served the multiple purposes of redistributing wealth, establishing social bonds, and demonstrating leadership through generosity. In Buddhism, the concept of dana (generosity) represents the first of the paramitas or "perfections" that followers seek to develop. The Dalai Lama emphasizes that "generosity is the most natural outward expression of an inner attitude of compassion and loving-kindness"—a teaching that suggests genuine generosity flows naturally from a heart that recognizes our common humanity.[51]

In Islam, zakat (charitable giving) stands as one of the five pillars of faith, while sadaqah (voluntary charity) is strongly encouraged. "The generous person is close to Allah," said the Prophet Muhammad. "Close to paradise, close to people, and far from hell." Of course, generosity is a fundamental Christian virtue as well. And the ancient Chinese concept of guanxi, which translates as "a closed caring system of relationships," emphasizes the importance of reciprocity and caring as a primary way of building social networks and maintaining harmony. This principle continues to influence broader social interactions throughout East Asia, demonstrating how traditional wisdom about reciprocity remains relevant in modern contexts.

The many faces of generosity

Generosity manifests in numerous ways beyond material giving. For example, in her work with indigenous communities, anthropologist Margaret Mead demonstrated that deep, attentive listening was one of the highest forms of generosity and relationship building. Her careful documentation and respectful attention to cultural practices helped bridge understanding between different societies, showing how Mead's ability to truly listen to others reflected the reverence she had for the people and their culture.[52]

Being heard and fully understood is one of the greatest gifts we can receive. It says "I matter. My existence has significance." Imagine the world we could have if every child on the planet grew up knowing that about themselves—or the children you encounter in your life or your friends and colleagues or, or, or ...

Knowledge sharing is another form of generosity. Junko Tabei, the first woman to reach the summit of Mount Everest and ascend the Seven Summits, climbing the highest peak on every continent, dedicated much of her life to environmental conservation and mentoring young climbers, particularly women. She established the Ladies Climbing Club in Japan to help break down gender barriers in mountaineering, showing how success creates opportunities for meaningful giving and lifting others up. And the world reciprocated her gifts. So far, she's had an asteroid named after her as well as a mountain range on the planet Pluto!

English anthropologist and primatologist Jane Goodall revolutionized our understanding of primates and knew that she could share her knowledge and skills to inspire the next generation of anthropologists. She created numerous programs to mentor young scientists and conservationists, especially women and girls in developing nations. Her Roots & Shoots program exemplifies how generously sharing experience and wisdom can inspire new generations to effectively make positive change happen.[53]

Of course, there truly are no greater gifts to give and receive than time and attention, which Mother Teresa's work in Calcutta amply demonstrated. Even if we have few or no material resources, we can still practice meaningful generosity through giving the gift of presence and hands-on interaction, as well as mentorship and guidance. This form of giving often creates ripple effects as beneficiaries pay forward the guidance they've received.

Giving and receiving

The principle of reciprocity appears to be hardwired into human psychology and social systems. In his seminal work *Influence: The Psychology of Persuasion,* Robert Cialdini, Professor Emeritus of Psychology and Marketing at Arizona State University, identifies reciprocity as one of the fundamental principles of human behavior.[54] When we receive something, we feel naturally inclined to give in return.

However, real giving isn't calculated or transactional.

> **Those who help others without expecting any return often achieve the greatest long-term success.**

That said, the research of University of Pennsylvania Wharton School professor in organizational psychology, Adam Grant, shows that genuine givers—those who help others without expecting any return—often achieve the greatest long-term success. Their generosity builds strong networks, establishes trust, and creates opportunities through genuine relationships.[55] It's as if life itself is paying attention and making sure genuine givers receive in turn.

Apparently, that's how the quantum field works. I've noticed that generosity with strings attached, expecting or hoping for something in return, makes that action less satisfying. Giving willingly from the heart feels good. Which is its own reward. As for getting in return, well, that may come from someone or something that had nothing to do with your original act of generosity. So don't be attached to whether it happens or what it may look like.

Consider the example of Gertrude Bell, the renowned English explorer, archaeologist, and diplomat whose generosity of spirit and cultural respect earned her unprecedented trust among Arab leaders in the early 20th century.

Generous leadership and cultural reciprocity can overcome seemingly insurmountable barriers.

By sharing her knowledge, respecting local customs, and maintaining genuine concern for the welfare of the people she encountered, she built important bridges between cultures in the Middle East.[56] Her example shows how generous leadership and cultural reciprocity can overcome seemingly insurmountable barriers.

The benefits of practicing generosity extend into the regions of mental health. Studies show that generous behavior triggers the release of oxytocin and other neurochemicals associated with positive emotions and reduced stress.[57] Regular giving activities correlate with improved mental health outcomes. Individuals and organizations that foster cultures of generosity and knowledge sharing typically demonstrate higher levels of innovation and creativity. There's also the added benefit of feelings of safety hanging out in an environment of shared ideas and helping others. Individual and collective intelligence flourishes. Communities that build strong reciprocal relationships demonstrate greater resilience in facing challenges. The same principle applies to individuals. Those with strong support networks built through generous behavior tend to bounce back more effectively from setbacks than those who don't have a support network.

The costs of withholding

While generosity and reciprocity build connections and create opportunities, their opposites—stinginess, greed, and failure to reciprocate—can exact heavy tolls. Research in organizational psychology shows that perceived greed and failure to reciprocate trust often leads to reduced cooperation and damaged relationships, diminished social capital and networking opportunities, lost opportunities for collaboration and growth, and reduced innovation. All of this leads to negative emotions and increased stress.

Historical examples abound of leaders and organizations whose focus on taking rather than giving led to their downfall. For example, the collapse of Enron Corporation, an

American-based energy, commodities, and services company based in Houston, Texas, profoundly demonstrates how a culture of greed and self-interest can ultimately destroy even seemingly invincible institutions. The company's fraudulent accounting practices were not the result of a few bad actors, but were instead a product of the company's culture of greed and deceit which permeated the organization and created an environment where ethical boundaries were blurred. A workplace environment where the end always justified the means, employees were not just permitted but encouraged to sidestep traditional ethical boundaries. Those who spoke out against the fraudulent practices were often ostracized or fired. Eventually the scandal came to light and, after posting claimed revenues of nearly $101 billion in the year 2000, Enron filed bankruptcy the following year, serving as a cautionary tale highlighting the importance of transparency, accountability, ethical leadership, and the need for robust corporate governance practices.[58]

Cultivating generosity

Generosity can be developed through conscious practice. Here are some practical approaches:

- **Learn from Role Models**: Study the examples of notably generous individuals in your field or community. How do they approach giving?
- **Start small**: Begin with simple acts of generosity in daily life, such as sharing knowledge, offering support, or simply giving your full attention to others when they speak.

- **Practice mindful giving**: Consider how your unique skills and resources might benefit others. What can you uniquely contribute to others around you?

- **Build giving habits**: Create regular opportunities for giving, whether through volunteering, mentoring, or supporting causes you care about.

- **Notice opportunities**: Train yourself to recognize moments where you can make a positive difference through generous action.

The practice of generosity and reciprocity represents a kind of adventure in itself, one that requires courage, wisdom, and a willingness to trust in the fundamental interconnectedness of human experience. Like adventure, it involves uncertainty and possible disappointment yet also offers the potential for amazing rewards—not just in terms of personal success or satisfaction, but in the profound sense of meaning that comes from contributing to the wellbeing of others.

Reflective questions

Ask yourself:

1. When in my life have I experienced unexpected generosity from another? How did it affect me? What specific moment did someone's generosity, whether of attention, time, resources, or money, have an impact on my path?

2. In my current relationships (personal and professional), where might I be taking more than I'm giving?

Conversely, where am I giving without allowing others the opportunity to reciprocate in healthy ways?

3. Generous actions can shift dynamics in unexpected ways. When have I witnessed generosity transform a difficult situation or relationship?

4. What would it look like to practice more generous listening in my key relationships? How might I create more space for others' perspectives and experiences, at home, at work, and out in the world?

5. What legacy of generosity would I like to create? If I look back in ten years, what impact would I like my actions to have had on others and my community?

PRINCIPLE #17

STEWARDSHIP: CARING FOR WHAT SUPPORTS AND SUSTAINS

You are a drop of water that ripples through centuries. Stand knowing that you are an ancestor of the future.

~ Luisah Teish

The dictionary definition of "stewardship" is: The careful and responsible management of something entrusted to one's care. The word "entrusted" seems significant here, as if to extract a promise from us to commit to do our best, to be our best, and to approach responsibilities with respect and reverence.

From a young age, my parents instilled in me the belief that it is my responsibility to be a good steward of the land. This understanding has progressed to the point where I now consider it my responsibility to be a good steward of the earth, taking into consideration the generations to come. This happens to be in alignment with indigenous cultures worldwide which embody sophisticated systems of stewardship that take into account how individual actions affect the whole over the long term. "Winning" is not individual in this view, but rather recast as collective thriving.

The earth makes life possible for humans and supports us in so many ways. In return, our stewardship should nurture, sustain, and restore that which supports us in this life. Unsurprisingly, the concept of stewardship appears as a fundamental value across diverse cultures and spiritual traditions, suggesting its universal importance to human flourishing. The Quechua people of the Andes revere Pachamama (Mother Earth) not as a resource to be exploited, but as a living being deserving of respect and the reciprocity of mutual support. The Haudenosaunee Confederacy requires decision-makers to consider how their choices will affect descendants seven generations into the future. As Chief Sealth, a 19th century leader of the Suquamish and Duwamish tribes in the Pacific Northwest put it, "We do not inherit the Earth from our ancestors; we borrow it from our children."

Stewarding organizations and people

Most enterprising leaders I've met who have led organizations that are successful over a long period of time attribute that longevity at least partly to a stewardship mindset that prioritized long-term sustainability over short-term gains.

Reduced costs through careful stewardship of resources— whether material, human, or financial—are typical as policies of resource utilization and reduced waste are implemented. People in organizations are inspired to be more *care-full* and mindful in their work when the company ethos is one of stewardship. Which brings me to the point about being a good steward of people as well as organizations.

There is an old business adage that goes: "People join a company, but they leave their manager." (You can replace the word manager with leader, CEO, Board of Directors, even an industry.) Which basically means that somewhere along the employment trajectory, there was a failure in human relationship, engagement, and motivation.

If an organization is attentive to stewardship, the leaders understand that they are entrusted with an employee's care in all areas, from recruitment to the exit interview. (Do not confuse this with the restrictive parental model of management "father knows best" which does not keep people engaged and excelling.) The culture of stewardship is driven by vision and purpose and executed by creating an environment rich in learning and opportunities, guidance, and healthy cross-team, cross-department, and cross-hierarchy interactions. Longer-term employment is standard in this model.

And yet, much too often we see employee's enthusiasm and sparkle fade after the initial employment period. The excited new-hire begins to quiet their voice and wait to be prompted to contribute. They arrive to meetings less than enthusiastic, late, or sometimes not at all. Sometimes this happens in a short time, sometimes it takes a few years. Unfortunately, leaders often miss these cues because they're too busy studying the numbers, vying for limited resources, strategizing how to keep the competition at bay, etc. Or they simply don't know what to do. I can't begin to count the number of organizational leaders I've heard say, "I'm not here to be a psychologist." Which means they simply avoid these situations until it becomes a performance issue. So, it's either 1) they don't see it; 2) they do see it but don't know how to approach the subject; or 3) they do see it but don't want to deal with it because what if they can't fix it? Leaders who take an active stewardship view of their role, however, automatically consider their peoples' wellbeing. These CEOs and managers have high noticing skills and listen deeply to what's being said and what's not being said. They get good at being curious, asking questions that invite others to be open and frank and not be afraid to think big. Some leaders say they don't have time to do this. But frankly, they don't have time *not* to do this if they want sustainable success.

Bottomline, all employer/employee interactions are teaching moments. Whether you know it or not, with every word you say and action you take, you are teaching people if you have time for them ... or not. You are teaching them what they can say and bring to you ... and not. You are teaching them how to treat others. Guidance and mentorship start with you and will pay dividends over time, not just for that one person, but for the many others down the line that they will guide as well.

Stewardship systems

The ancient Hawaiians *ahupua'a* land division system represents one of history's most sophisticated approaches to environmental stewardship at a systems level. Based upon the principle of resource sustainability and *malama aina* or "care of the land," traditional land divisions ran from *mauka* to *makai*—from the mountain peaks to the sea—following the natural boundaries of watersheds. Rather than one group warring with others to take over the best arable land for itself, leaving others to eke out a subsistence living on less fertile soils, this system recognized that in order to thrive, each group needed access to upland forests, agricultural zones, and coastal areas, enabling sustainable resource management that could support large populations indefinitely.

Similarly, the Balinese *subak* system, established around the 9th century and recognized by UNESCO as a World Heritage site, demonstrates how traditional wisdom can create sustainable agricultural practices through careful water management and social cooperation. In this 49,000 acre system managed by hundreds of small farmers, forests protect and funnel the water supply into a system of canals, ponds, and tunnels, all of which pass through temples of varying size and importance on its way downhill to irrigate the rice paddies. A cooperative system of sustainable water management, *subak* has shaped and balanced the landscape while sustaining dozens of communities for over a thousand years.

Self-care as stewardship

A little-recognized aspect of stewardship is self-care. Personal well-being is not self-indulgence, but rather responsible stewardship of our most basic resource—ourselves. Successful adventurers understand this.

Personal well-being is not self-indulgence, but rather responsible stewardship of our most basic resource — ourselves.

American polar explorer Ann Bancroft emphasizes this principle. "You have to be your own best advocate and steward of your capabilities," she says. Her meticulous attention to physical preparation through proper nutrition, rest, and training, mental conditioning through stress management and emotional awareness, building resilience through gradual challenge exposure, team skill development, and continuous learning team dynamics underlie her expedition successes.[59] The Ann Bancroft foundation started in 1991 supports the Wilderness Inquiry group where Bancroft currently teaches these and other stewardship principles.

Stewardship in modern adventure

There is nothing more disheartening than trekking through the wilds of nature, basking in the pristine air and waters, admiring the untouched landscape, and coming upon a plastic candy wrapper tossed aside by a previous hiker. Or finding a burned-out fire ring filled with trash. In those moments it feels like, and represents, nothing less than a failure of stewardship and accountability by those who, with care-less-ness, walked those paths before us.

If I feel that way hiking the Cascade Trail, how much more devastating is it for climbers arduously fighting for breath ascending peaks like Annapurna, the 10th highest mountain in Nepal, to stumble across emptied supply cartons and broken equipment—the detritus of climbers from the past left behind them? This desecration—for that is what it is—has exponentially increased over the years as more and more people living in sterile city and suburban landscapes seek revitalization through adventure.

Fortunately, the trashing of the wild places has initiated a huge movement towards greater stewardship, marked by the development of biodegradable packaging, more ecologically friendly equipment and more ecofriendly exploratory practices, like using solar chargers to replace disposable batteries, eco-friendly camping gear made from recycled materials, and biodegradable soaps that don't damage pristine waters

"Pack it in, pack it out" has become the motto of modern adventuring. "Leave no trace" principles have been developed to reduce the environmental impact from hikers and campers, including traveling and camping on trails and sites that have been used before. If forced off trail, hikers are encouraged to travel and camp on hard surfaces where possible, leaving the surrounding ecosystems undamaged. Campfires are replaced with portable cooking stoves and all who come are now advised to leave natural objects alone. Hikers are urged to take pictures of rocks, plants, and found objects like pottery shards if they must. But to leave them in place for others to discover and enjoy. And to never feed wildlife because it alters their natural behavior, harms their health, and makes them aggressive with humans.

Outdoor groups now sponsor clean-up days, tree planting events, and educational workshops designed to teach people how to preserve and give back to nature while affording the opportunity to meet like-minded people. Stewardship is now an accepted value and practice throughout the outdoor community. Now if we could just get the rest of the world onboard!

> *The trashing of the wild places has initiated a huge movement towards greater stewardship, marked by the development of biodegradable packaging, more ecologically friendly equipment and more ecofriendly exploratory practices.*

The triple bottom line

Developed in 1994 by British corporate responsibility and sustainable development authority John Elkington, the triple bottom line of people, planet and profits, aka the 3Ps or the TBL, has become part of everyday business language and a practical business framework for measuring and reporting corporate performance against social, environmental, and economic parameters.

In the simplest terms, the TBL agenda focuses corporations not just on the economic value that they add, but also on the environmental and social value that they add—or destroy. As Elkington writes: "With its dependence on seven closely linked 'revolutions,' the sustainable capitalism transition will be one of the most complex our species has ever had to negotiate as we move into the third millennium." These seven "revolutions" identified by Elkington mark a radical shift from the old business paradigm to the new. They include a shift from 1) Markets: Compliance → Competition, 2) Values: Hard → Soft; 3) Transparency: Closed → Open; 4) Life-cycle technology: Product → Function; 5) Partnerships: Subversion → Symbiosis; 6) Time: Wider → Longer; and finally, 7) Corporate governance: Exclusive → Inclusive.

"It is clear that a growing proportion of corporate sustainability issues revolve not just around process and product design, but also around the design of corporations and their value chains, of 'business ecosystems' and, ultimately, of markets," he says. "Experience suggests that the best way to ensure that a given corporation fully addresses the TBL agenda is to build the relevant requirements into its corporate DNA from the very outset—and into the parameters of the markets that it seeks to serve."[60]

A stewardship revolution indeed! A revolution that is still struggling to be birthed. On the 25th anniversary of the TBL framework (2019), Elkington publicly stated that it was time to do a "strategic recall" of the term. The triple bottom line had become synonymous in business lexicon to mean the measurement of financial, social, and environmental performance of a corporation.

Many early adopters understood the concept as a balancing act, adopting a trade-off mentality.[61] But the TBL wasn't designed to be just an accounting tool. It was supposed to provoke deeper thinking about capitalism and its future.

TBL's stated goal from the outset was *system change*—pushing toward the transformation of capitalism itself. In essence, Elkington's TBL framework was intended to move corporations toward stewardship of this transformation. But he hasn't lost hope. He sees potential in the increase in the number of certified B-Corps dedicated to being "best *for* the world."[62]

Unfortunately, the majority of corporate leaders have yet to wrap their heads around the fact that stewardship and cooperation (versus ruthless exploitation and killing the competition) most often lead to greater abundance for all rather than scarcity and economic hierarchy. A truth that, as we have seen, has been proven over and over again throughout history by indigenous and spiritual cultures the world over. A truth the Greek fabulist and storyteller Aesop pointed out in the 6th century BCE as follows:

"There was once a Countryman who possessed the most wonderful Goose you can imagine, for every day when he visited the nest, the Goose had laid a beautiful, glittering, golden egg. The Countryman took the eggs to market and soon began to get rich. But it was not long before he grew impatient with the Goose because she gave him only a single golden egg a day. He was not getting rich fast enough.

Then one day, after he had finished counting his money, the idea came to him that he could get all the golden eggs at once by killing the Goose and cutting it open. But when the deed was done, not a single golden egg did he find, and his precious Goose was dead."[63]

Whether applied to adventure, our organizations, or daily life, the principle of wise stewardship, offers a powerful framework for sustainable success. It reminds us that our achievements depend not just on our actions but on our careful attention to the systems and relationships that support us.

As modern society grapples with environmental challenges and resource limitations, the ancient wisdom of stewardship becomes increasingly relevant. Careful stewardship not only preserves resources but often enhances our ability to achieve our goals and to not just survive but thrive.

Reflective questions:

1. Consider a team or organization that you are part of: Where does stewardship show up? In what form?

What is in need of stewardship? How could applying stewardship practices strengthen its long-term sustainability and success? What specific practices or changes might you suggest?

2. Reflect on your most important relationships (personal, professional, or in adventure settings). How might approaching these relationships through the lens of stewardship—careful tending and nurturing—change how you interact?

3. What wisdom from your own cultural or family traditions about stewardship resonates with you? How might you apply this wisdom more intentionally in your life and work?

4. If you were to create a "stewardship manifesto" for your family or future generations about caring for themselves, their relationships, and their environment, what key ideas would you include? Why?

5. What systems or practices do you currently benefit from that were thoughtfully stewarded by previous generations? How might you expand or enhance these for the benefit of those who follow?"

PRINCIPLE # 18

SEEK WISDOM: DISCERNMENT, CURIOSITY, CONTINUOUS LEARNING, & CRITICAL THINKING

Blessed are those who find wisdom, those who gain understanding.

~ Proverbs 3:13

Ancient teachings of every culture encourage us to, first and foremost, cultivate wisdom by seeking to understand ourselves and our relationship with the world around us. From the Delphic Oracle's maxim "Know thyself" to the Buddhist emphasis on mindful awareness, the acquisition of wisdom through patient observation, honest self-reflection, discernment, curiosity, and openness to learning from all sources, shines forth as the only possible answer to humanity safely navigating the complexities and ramifications of the exponential technological growth we're experiencing in our world today.

So far in this book we have examined most of the wisdom teachings from around the world and gleaned their lessons.

The need for balance and harmony taught in the Taoist texts. The Zen power of being present in the moment or being in the "now" as modern spiritual teacher Eckhart Tolle puts it. The need to accept change as a constant. The illusion of separation and the truth that all things are connected, which *everybody* from the Buddha to the Sufi poet Rumi to quantum physicists talk about. The importance of community and the necessity of maintaining integrous values while following a purpose greater than simply service to self. The need for authenticity, gratitude and generosity.

Every single one of these qualities is a hallmark of wisdom. Indeed, the qualities a person expresses reveal wisdom as being a cumulative effect of embodied virtue rather than a "thing" in itself. And to the list of virtues that add up to wisdom expressed by a human being, I would like to add the relevance of discernment and open-minded curiosity.

The importance of discernment

Discernment is the ability to perceive and comprehend subtle details and information in people and situations that are often obscure and missed by most. It's a matter of insight and the ability to perceive subtle differences and make sound judgments; to pick up on patterns and nuances that others don't easily recognize; to recognize what's important and what is not. As you can imagine, discernment can make the difference between life and death on a mountainside, and is a vital ingredient in the adventure mindset.

Take, for instance, the remarkable story of Junko Tabei, the first woman to summit Mount Everest. Prior to her historic climb, Tabei spent years studying not only modern climbing techniques but also traditional Sherpa wisdom about the mountain. She discerned that local knowledge, passed down through generations, could provide insights that no modern guidebook could offer. Her curiosity and openness to learning from different cultural perspectives allowed Junko to discern which actions to take, when to move, when to stay put on the expedition, and proved crucial to her success and survival.[64]

Contrast this with the sobering example of Sir John Franklin who failed to discern the importance of learning local Inuit knowledge about Arctic survival techniques. That, and his unwillingness to adapt British naval traditions to Arctic conditions, led to the loss of two ships and 129 lives on the Franklin Expedition of 1845.[65]

In the world of business, government, or other organizations, discernment can inform the type of questions you ask in a contract negotiation to get just the right information you need. Discernment can help you choose the right person for a job. And developing this ability requires you to use your awareness muscle. It requires quieting the chatter in your brain. It requires a certain level of "not knowing" in order not to miss seeing the subtle nuances that can provide a more complete understanding of something or someone.

Few sayings point out the relationship between discernment and wisdom as well as the Serenity Prayer picked up from an unknown source by Alcoholics Anonymous back in the 1930s. It has permeated society with its relevance:

> *God grant me the serenity to accept the things*
> *I cannot change; courage to change the things I can;*
> *and wisdom to know the difference.*

Being able to discern what I can change and what I cannot; discerning which path to take and which *not* to take, what action to initiate or hold back on, what words to speak or withhold—discernment is probably one of the most important qualities any explorer or entrepreneur could possibly hope to develop in their pursuit of excellence and wisdom.

Curiosity as the catalyst of evolution

Twentieth century American motivational author William Arthur Ward once said: "Curiosity is the wick in the candle of learning."[66] And he was right. Curiosity has driven humankind forward perhaps more than any other human quality. From "What's around the next bend in the river?" to "I wonder what this venison haunch would taste like if we hung it over the fire?" to "What kind of vehicle can get us to the moon?" curiosity has been the impulse behind every innovation and discovery mankind has ever made. Certainly, it has always been the wick in the candle of exploration!

> **"Curiosity is the wick in the candle of learning."**

"Can I do it? Can we do it? Can we scale that cliff? Ascend that peak? What does it look like from up there? How far can we see? What's on the other side of this ocean? What's at the bottom of this cave? What's on the other side of this ice field? Where does this river lead? Is it possible to climb that without ropes? Without supplemental oxygen?" And on and on.

In the realm of innovation and invention, no historical figure embodied curiosity more than Leonardo da Vinci. His relentless curiosity and joy in discovery led him to study everything from human anatomy to bird flight, from water flow to light reflection. As Walter Isaacson notes in his biography *Leonardo da Vinci*, Leonardo's genius stemmed not from innate talent alone but from his insatiable curiosity and willingness to question everything. He would spend days observing the way water swirled around obstacles, making detailed notes and drawings that would later inform his engineering projects.

One particularly illustrative example comes from Leonardo's study of human flight. Rather than simply designing flying machines based on emulating the way birds achieve flight, he meticulously studied bird wings, air currents, and the principles of wind resistance and lift and then applied those observations by engineering machines that incorporated what he learned. And while his flying machines never achieved success in his lifetime, his methodical approach to understanding the natural phenomena of flight set the foundation for modern aerodynamics.[67]

Curiosity in the workplace

American billionaire businessman Michael Saul Dell, founder, chairman, and CEO of Dell Technologies, once responded to a question on an investor survey asking what character trait he thought was most aligned with success. "I would place my bet on curiosity," he responded.

Encouraging inquisitiveness and out-of-the-box thinking helps organizations adapt to uncertain market conditions and external pressures, augmenting the chance of an organization's success.

Studies show that people with an open, curious mind are less likely to fall prey to confirmation bias. As well, people who are curious tend not to stereotype people and situations as much as others.[68] All of which is highly useful in the marketplace when organizational success often depends upon looking for and discovering alternative views, approaches and solutions to the status quo.

Austrian-American management consultant, educator, and author Peter Drucker, known to many as the Father of Modern Management, placed a high value on workers who were curious and asked questions, who could solve problems by thinking creatively—a vitally important approach that is becoming more and more important as the world increases in complexity.[69]

The ability to learn from diverse perspectives is also essential. I've heard it said that the sign of a good culture is one that is accepting of another culture, and have found that the most successful organizations and expeditions are those that are led by people who actively seek out and embrace diverse viewpoints.

American hedge fund manager and author, Ray Dalio, founder of Bridgewater Associates, and proponent of what he calls "radical open-mindedness," contends that the ability to examine one's own beliefs critically, consider alternative viewpoints, and then discern what learned information to apply isn't just helpful—it's essential for success.[70] As Abraham Lincoln famously stated after winning re-election in 1864 with just 55 percent of the popular vote, "I will try to understand why so many people disagreed with me."[71] This willingness to understand opposing viewpoints, even in times of extreme conflict like the America Civil War, exemplifies the wisdom of being curious and seeking to understand what's going on behind situations and outcomes rather than merely accepting what is happening at face value.

Creating environments that nurture wisdom

For leaders of corporations and leaders of expeditions, creating an environment where curiosity, questions and learning can flourish requires wisdom and intentional effort. This means establishing psychological safety where team members feel secure in expressing dissenting views, raising concerns, or positing an audacious idea.

It's not a simple matter to point fingers at organizational leaders, economic conditions, and specific market situations where a lack of psychological safety and questioning led directly to a failure. But in our age of information and misinformation abundance, the path of wisdom requires careful attention to the quality of our information sources and the ability to question those sources. Successful leaders and adventurers must rely on verified data and scientific understanding while remaining open to new information that might challenge their existing beliefs.

What are the best practices for developing greater and greater wisdom? Well, modestly, I suggest cultivating as many of the adventure principles set forth in this book as possible. Life is the biggest adventure in the universe. And a life well-lived is a result of acquiring wisdom through lived experiences that teach us the value of embodying the principles of harmony, oneness, awareness, authenticity, inspiration, purpose, etc.

Seek wisdom with these practices:

- **Practice deliberate curiosity:** Learning something new can be as simple as asking "why" and "how" questions about everyday phenomena. Follow your natural curiosity and intentionally explore topics that challenge your existing worldview.

- **Cultivate deep listening:** When engaging with others, focus on understanding rather than judging. Pay attention to non-verbal cues and emotional content. Create space for others to share their complete thoughts before responding.

- **Seek diverse perspectives:** Actively build relationships with people who can add to your viewpoint. Now, that doesn't mean they always agree with your viewpoint or you theirs. The point is inviting perspectives from different expertise, backgrounds, cultures, and belief systems. Read books by authors whose experiences differ from yours. Participate in cross-cultural exchanges and diverse community events. Challenge yourself to understand viewpoints that conflict with your own. Make sure your team believes you when you say "I want to know what you think."

- **Don't shoot the messenger:** When you get information or feedback you don't like or would rather not hear, pause, re-orient yourself, and go deeper into the conversation. Seek to understand, not react.

- **Learn from experiences:** After any significant event or decision, conduct a personal or team after-action review. Start with "How did it go? How do you feel?" Then ask the more typical questions of "What went well? What could have gone better?" and "What's the wisdom we want to capture?"

- **Create a way to track** the outcomes of your decisions and analyze patterns over time.

- **Balance action and reflection:** Combine practical experience with contemplative practice. Take action to test your understanding, then step back to process the results. Create regular intervals for both active learning and quiet reflection.

- **Build wisdom collectives:** Develop relationships with mentors and peers who share your commitment to growth and learning. Create or join study groups, discussion circles, or learning communities. Share your own insights while remaining open to feedback and alternative perspectives.

- **Curate your own wisdom collection:** Record insights, questions, and lessons learned. Review past experiences—the wins and the failures and challenges—to extract deeper understanding. Record questions that arise and revisit them periodically.

Conclusion

The pursuit of wisdom and all the traits that add up to wisdom, while ancient in origin, has relevancy in our complex modern world. Each generation is tempted to bypass "wisdom" in favor of "going their own way." What is not understood here is that wisdom is organic, not finite. Learning from the learning of others, of generations, of cultures, even of the earth, combined with learning from your own endeavors, is an opportunity to open your spirit to the infinite possibility that is wisdom.

Wisdom demands that we remain students throughout our lives, ready to learn from every experience and every encounter with humility, courage, and persistence. In doing so, we not only enhance our own capabilities but contribute to the collective wisdom that will live on and evolve as future generations live their own adventures and discoveries.

Reflective Questions

1. How do I typically react when encountering ideas that challenge my existing beliefs?
2. What practices, habits, or mindsets currently support or hinder my pursuit of wisdom?
3. How could a more systematic approach to learning from experience, especially failures, benefit my team or organization?
4. What systems or practices could I implement to better capture and share wisdom within my organization?
5. What role does curiosity play in my approach to adventure and exploration both physical and metaphorical?
6. How can I create an environment where team members (including family members!) feel safe sharing concerns and alternative viewpoints during critical situations?

PRINCIPLE #19

MINDFUL CREATIVITY, INNOVATION, AND "SOMETHING ELSE" ...

Creativity requires the courage to let go of certainties.

~ Eric Fromm

Mindful creativity is an adventure—a journey of continuous learning and exploration. It requires courage to challenge existing paradigms while maintaining respect for the knowledge that has brought us this far. It demands both rootedness and openness, technical skill and imaginative vision. Mindful creativity is not a passive process but an active, intentional engagement with the physical world around us and the non-physical realms of information. It requires us to be fully present, to listen deeply—to data, to diverse perspectives, to the whispers of traditional wisdom, to the emergent possibilities that lie just beyond our current understanding, and to the voices of pure inspiration.

At its core, mindful creativity is about exploration. It is a holistic approach that recognizes innovation not as a rejection of the past, but as a thoughtful dialogue between what has been and what could be. It also includes an acceptance and invitation to that which we cannot yet imagine—like an experienced mountaineer who respects the terrain while charting a novel path.

A good example of mindful creativity, innovation, and "something else" is indigenous navigation techniques. For thousands of years Polynesian wayfinders traversed vast oceanic expanses, accomplishing navigational feats that are truly remarkable. A testament to their deep understanding of the natural world and their incredible seamanship, they navigated one of the Earth's largest and most challenging environments without the aid of modern instruments like compasses or GPS, using a sophisticated synthesis of accumulated generational wisdom, creative thinking, adaptation to moment-to-moment observations, all combined with pure, unadulterated gut "knowing."

Key aspects of their navigation techniques included:

- **Star navigation**: They possessed an intimate knowledge of the night sky, including the rising and setting points of hundreds of stars, using a "star compass," an imaginary mental map of the sky, to determine their latitude (north-south position) and maintain their course. This required exceptional spatial reasoning, memory, and the ability to integrate multiple sources of information.

- **Observation of nature**: The understood the messages contained within the flight patterns of various birds, cloud formations, and the behavior of marine animals.

- **Water reading:** They understood wave and swell patterns and the ocean currents, recognizing those generated by local conditions versus those originating from distant storms or landmasses thousands of miles away.

- **Creativity and adaptiveness:** Polynesian navigation required constant adaptation and creative response to environmental cues, as well as the ability to let absolutely everything go and trust inner guidance.

- **Gut knowing and something else:** We're all familiar with the sense of knowing something without any basis for knowing it. We call it gut instinct, and Polynesian navigators had it in abundance. But they also had something else: *They stayed completely present to the experience and the present moment.*

They allowed every moment to carry them to the next moment and the next place and the next decision. They were vulnerable with uncertainty and humble in their "not knowing," which created mental, psychological, and emotional spaciousness for "something else"—non-linear information—to show up. They trusted their instincts and trusted life itself to guide their journey and provide what they needed.

This "something else" doesn't lend itself to intellectual understanding or normal doing. It is a level of creativity that has *nothing* to do with knowledge, tradition, adaptation, imaginative thinking, talent, the gut, or anything else humans are usually familiar and comfortable with. The best way I can explain is to give you an example.

I have a friend who is a writer. Back in her school days she was working on her master's degree in psychology, and she was in the midst of taking a final exam taught by the head of the department on the "Nature of Creativity." This particular professor gave exams by passing a hat with questions in it. Students would draw a question, then have an hour of open book prep before coming together to discuss their answers. Exams were held in a student's home, and often lasted through the night.

She told me what she drew out of the hat wasn't a question, it was "Write an epic poem or short story depicting the psychological and emotional evolution of mankind through the last 5000 years." She told me she totally freaked out at the impossibility of the task, but that when she asked, the professor wouldn't let her pick another topic. Resigned to getting an "F" on her exam, she grabbed a pen and paper, stomped out of the house out onto her front lawn (the exam was being held at her house), and set about trying to come up with a story. And failed utterly.

She said that after an exasperating half hour of trying, she stopped. It was impossible! She got angry. Then she cried. Finally, she gave up, closed her notebook, and lay down on the grass and closed her eyes. And after a few minutes ... a story appeared, full-blown in her mind, complete with an exciting plot, names, places, backstory, a protagonist, developmental character arcs ... the whole nine yards.

At that point she had about ten minutes to write the story down. But that wasn't the exciting part or even the point. The exam was on the nature of creativity. And she'd just been given first-hand experience of a level of creativity she hadn't even known existed. At the outset of the test, she'd tried her damnedest to figure a story out. To come up with something with her mind the old-fashioned way and had come up with nothing. Nada. And then BAM! There it was. A complete creation springing from nothing—or what seemed like nothing. What, she wondered, had happened?

Something else.

It is a mystery to my friend that, to this day, she cannot logically explain. Personally, I believe she tapped into the creative instinct that is ours for the "allowing" that is often buried deep as if forbidden. Letting go of the narrative she was wrapped in and allowing there to be *nothing* until there was *something*.

All humans, potentially, have the creative capacity to call on ... I'm not sure what—God? Nature? Life intelligence? The Universe? Zero point energy?—in a time of great need. And apparently sometimes SOMETHING happens. Something is created in answer to the need that meets the need exactly. Spontaneous generation? I don't know. Magic? Seems like it. But I bring this up because there are legends of early Polynesian navigators doing something very like what my friend did—create something from nothing through no known process whatsoever. And this creation isn't limited to stories and ideas. In the case of Polynesian wayfinders, some had life-saving landfalls simply "appear" when a landfall should have been impossible by any and all known means.

As mentioned under the principle of inspiration, many of the greatest inventions and breakthroughs in history have

> *As far as human creative capacity is concerned it seems the sky is not the limit.*

come through some amount of inspiration. But what, exactly, is inspiration? How does it work? What brings it forth? It is said the only impossible thing is a closed mind. The suggestion I am making here is: As far as human creative capacity is concerned it seems the sky is not the limit.

The power of intention

Of course, what I've left out of the equation in the story above is intention. Intention is the foundation for all creation, the old-fashioned linear kind and the inexplicable kind. Every choice we make in life flows from an intention and is an opportunity to not only bring mindfulness into the creative process, but to open ourselves up to the potential of unknown potential.

The intention to go beyond the known is grounded in a mindset of genuine curiosity and humility, as well as a willingness to experience different ways of perceiving and expressing ourselves. Consider how explorers throughout history have approached unknown territories. The most successful were not those who imposed their existing knowledge onto new landscapes, but those who remained deeply observant, willing to learn from others, adaptive to changing circumstances, and openminded to unheard of possibilities. An approach requiring a delicate balance of confidence and vulnerability.

Which brings to mind a quote from Richard Branson, Founder at Virgin Group: "I've said it before and I'll say it again—dyslexia is a different way of seeing the world; a different way of solving problems. My biggest and most important message to all kids is that being different will be your biggest asset. Embrace your uniqueness, and you will fly." He also said this about business and creativity: "A business has to be involving, it has to be fun, and it has to exercise your creative instincts. And remember that happiness is the secret ingredient for successful businesses. If you have focus on keeping your people happy, your company will be invincible."[72]

In the end, mindful creativity is about maintaining a sense of wonder. It's about approaching each challenge as an opportunity for learning, each obstacle as a potential gateway to transformative insight. It invites us to be both explorers and stewards, innovators and preservers, always moving forward while remaining deeply connected to the rich tapestry of human knowledge, experience ... and mystery.

Reflective questions

1. **Creative curiosity self-assessment:**

    Ask yourself: When was the last time I approached a challenge with genuine curiosity rather than predetermined solutions? What stopped me from being more open to alternative perspectives or methods?

2. **Intentional choice challenge:**

    Identify a current project or ongoing challenge. What unconscious assumptions are driving your current approach? What might change if you deliberately questioned these assumptions and explored alternative perspectives?

3. **Creative courage reflection:**

   What innovative idea or approach have you been hesitant to pursue for fear of failure or judgment? What would it take for you to move from hesitation to intentional exploration?

4. **Personal innovation ecosystem:**

   Map out the sources of wisdom, learning, and inspiration in your life. Where are the potential blind spots? How can you intentionally diversify your sources of knowledge and creative input?

PRINCIPLE# 20

CONFIDENT HUMILITY AND INNER SECURITY

*Humility forms the basis of honor,
just as the low ground forms the foundation of a
high elevation.*

~ Bruce Lee

The very best leaders I've worked with are secure enough to admit when they don't know something. And they have a habit of asking a lot of questions. Along this vein, I can't help but think of Sally Jewell, a woman I was most fortunate to work for early in my career while she was still in commercial banking. At first, I wondered why she asked so many questions, especially when some of the questions she asked seemed elementary. What I learned was she had a strong background in science and technology and often had answers to the questions she was asking, *but was committed to checking her assumptions* and the information she'd gathered as a way of testing the solidity of her decisions the way any good scientist would.

She was brilliant and humble and concerned with what would work for the company and those who worked there. If doing that meant looking like she didn't know it all, that was fine with her. She also had the confidence and courage to make decisions and recommendations that were unpopular with some people around her, including people she reported to. Not surprisingly, she went on to many important leadership roles, serving as CEO of Recreational Equipment Inc., a multi-billion-dollar outdoor recreation equipment company, and numerous other leadership roles in high profile organizations. She uses her experience as a business executive and public servant to focus on supporting a robust economy coupled with long-term sustainability of our natural world and its diverse people.

Confidence versus arrogance

True strength comes from knowing both one's capabilities and limitations combined with a willingness to be curious — the end result being confident humility.

True strength comes from knowing both one's capabilities and limitations combined with a willingness to be curious—the end result being confident humility. Sally Jewell was the epitome of this. The ancient Chinese philosopher Lao Tzu wrote, "He who knows does not speak. He who speaks does not know." Who hasn't been on the receiving end of someone loudly bragging about what they know, only to later discover what they knew was incorrect or inapplicable to the situation or overexaggerated in the extreme? Meanwhile the quiet ones in the background get the job done.

Understanding the nuanced difference between confidence based in experience and ability and arrogance based in self-inflated ego is crucial for all of us. The key distinction lies not just in behavior but in underlying mindset. Confident individuals operate from a growth mindset, viewing challenges as opportunities to learn and improve. Arrogant individuals typically operate from a fixed mindset, seeing every interaction as a chance to prove their superiority. (It's difficult, but, if you can, have compassion for these people. That doesn't mean to accept the arrogant behavior. Just see it and them differently. Likely, someone, sometime in their life, told them they didn't matter. So, they have to prove that they do, over and over again. The irony is that the behavior they use to try to convince you they matter is the very behavior that makes you recoil and dismiss them. It's a vicious cycle.)

Anyway, true confidence emerges from a recognition of one's strengths and limitations, a willingness to acknowledge and learn from mistakes and successes, your own and others'. Arrogance, by contrast, can be recognized by one's resistance to feedback or criticism, dismissal of others' perspectives and expertise, overestimation of one's abilities without supporting evidence, the need to consistently prove superiority, and the tendency to blame external factors for failures.

In both corporate and adventure leadership contexts, arrogance poses particular danger by impairing decision-making and degrading your effectiveness and team dynamics while setting up missed opportunities for learning, growth and improvement. Arrogant over-estimation of capabilities in critical situations on an expedition, can get people killed.

Ed Viesturs is the first American to climb all fourteen 8,000-meter peaks around the world and the fifth person to do so without using supplemental oxygen. He completed his quest on May 12, 2005 with his ascent of Annapurna, one of the world's most treacherous peaks. But it took him 21 summiting attempts to accomplish this feat. He gave up on seven of those expeditions because conditions became too risky to proceed. One of those ascents he turned back just 300 feet from the summit of Mount Everest because weather conditions had turned blindingly dangerous.

His famous motto "Climbing has to be a round trip—summiting is optional, but descending is mandatory" reflects both the confidence needed to attempt such ambitious goals and the humility to recognize when conditions demand retreat. "It's OK. It's not a failure," he said in a 2016 interview for *Time* magazine. "We call it listening to the mountain. The mountain decides what you get to do. That's something that you really have to listen to. If you're rushing, if you're thinking it has to happen today, then you're going to make bad decisions."[73]

An adventure in confident humility

Back in the early 1980s, I spent three months in South America traveling by bus and train from one town to the next, going the length of the Andes mountains from Punta Arenas in Chile to Bogota, Columbia in the north. I had two objectives for this trip: Make photographs and improve my Spanish language skills.

Rather than have a 35mm film camera around my neck that might label me a tourist, (while producing mediocre images), I took along a large 8 x10 view camera that I'd built a few years earlier. I was enamored with the photography of Ansel Adams and other outdoor photographers, and they preferred this type of camera because of the large sheet film negatives that enabled very high resolution and sharpness in the photographs. Each sheet of film was nearly the size of a letter-sized sheet of paper. The camera's film holders could hold only two film sheets which had to be changed after every two exposures. But if it was a good enough setup for Ansel Adams and Edward Weston to make their classic and beloved photographs, it was worth it to me to put out the extra effort.

Needless to say, carrying an 8 x10 view camera prompted constant curiosity from the locals who readily engaged me in conversations that definitely helped improve my Spanish. I'd be setting up this clunky, old-style wooden camera on its tripod somewhere in a town and consistently be approached with smiles and questions like *"Que tipa de machina es esta?"* I met people from all segments of society this way: Rich, poor, young, old, from all walks of life and occupations— including the military when I was traveling through countries with military dictatorships in place.

As I traveled, I was keenly aware of potential revolutionary activities and civil unrest. Some train stations had extra security, and often buses I was riding would come upon a checkpoint where everyone would be ordered off the bus for a search of our bags and personal effects. The first time this happened, we were all told to put both hands against the side of the bus and stand there, legs spread, while they searched us and our bags. A bit unsettling to say the least! I never did get completely comfortable with it. And apparently nobody else really did either. I noticed many of the peasants/campesinos didn't fully trust the military and seemed wary of falling under extra scrutiny or worse.

As a foreigner, I didn't know all the nuances of these situations or what to expect. So, I kept my "awareness antennas" highly engaged. I focused on staying present and calm, all the while trying to take in the scenic countryside, much of which was as scary as the soldiers. As buses would climb the steep mountain roads into and through the low clouds, I'd be looking out the window at what must surely be a two-thousand-foot drop or more. Often the wheels were so close to the edge I couldn't see even an inch of shoulder between us and certain death—just a majorly disconcerting drop into a deep valley view below.

One day I got off the bus in a pleasant town in a nice setting just on the edge of where dramatic mountain slopes meet the flat valley floor. I climbed to a hilltop in the north part of town, my cumbersome camera in tow. Before the top of the hill, I paused to change the film sheets, and, as I was in the midst of restocking my film holders inside the dark changing bag to avoid light exposure, I noticed activity in the small military compound at the base of the hill. In fact, a military officer was looking through binoculars straight in my direction, checking me out.

Maybe it was the retrofitted US Army surplus backpack I was carrying or my green trousers and socks that got them worried. (Although the red suspenders holding my pants up should have shouted "Civilian!") But minutes after I made it to the top of the hill and was talking with some kids about the camera's upside-down image on the ground-glass, two soldiers carrying automatic rifles appeared, sweating and a bit out of breath. Then two more soldiers showed up from the opposite side of the hill. Between one sentence and the next, the kids vanished.

At that point, I realized I was about to get a free escorted tour to wherever they wanted to take me. I hefted the camera onto my shoulder and they marched me down the hill and in through the main gates of the local army brigade. Some off-duty guys were playing basketball in front of one of the buildings. The soldiers escorting me checked the contents of my small bag containing two film holders, film sheets, and one box of 75 sheets of exposed film. It was my last three weeks' worth of work, and I prayed they wouldn't open it and ruin all the film—as if that was the worst thing that could happen! The only other thing I was carrying was the journal I'd been keeping for the past couple months.

I was escorted to an office where a gentle older officer asked me some questions in English. He was intelligent and polite, and seemed to be some sort of quartermaster. By this point, a small crowd of young enlisted soldiers had gathered at the open doorway to listen. So, even though he had much better English than my Spanish, I decide to give my answers in Spanish for the benefit of the small crowd. I'm not sure why I did this other than a desire for the rank-and-file soldiers to understand that I was not a threat. I wanted to protect my film work and preserve my own safety, and my instincts had me trying to make friends with the old soldier as well as the young ones in the doorway. Hopefully, stumbling along in bad Spanish made me appear less risky.

But then I was ushered to the intelligence department for the *real* interrogation. I did my best to relax my mind and tune into the basic absurdity of this day, and almost began enjoying the encounters I was having with these army guys. Almost. I knew if I stayed relaxed, they would have less reason to be tense. And I maintained that tone of relaxation while cautioning myself from being too jovial—which might equally ring some alarm bells.

I explained my Andes photography project, and showed them how the camera worked. (It reminded me of a similar extemporaneous dissertation delivered in the freight yard supervisor's office of the Santa Fe Railroad one December day in Los Angeles. Making friends with the authorities seemed like a good idea then as well).

At one point they offered me a cup of coffee. I quickly calculated the risk that the coffee might be spiked with a drug that would have me waking up in some prison cell somewhere and balanced it against the possible ramifications of perceived rudeness if I refused. (I was fully aware of how important their country's famed coffee was to them. I'd passed many miles of coffee plantations on the way to this town.) It was a tough decision. But I was determined to continue the process of making friends with the hopes of demonstrating they had nothing to fear from me. So, I accepted the coffee, and it was smooth and rich as coffee should be. I complimented them on how good the coffee tasted and they offered a second cup, but I didn't want to press my luck any further and declined.

The questioning continued for several more hours, and I continued to exude friendliness the whole time. Gradually their initial suspicions that I was a spy of some sort was overcome. I mean, what spy in their right mind would be lugging around a conspicuous camera like that? After more conversation I was told I had to wait for the main man, "El jefe" the "boss," to see me before I could leave. But after a couple more hours in that office talking about my journey through the Andes, and the beautiful landscapes I'd seen and the nice people I'd met, letting their interpreter practice his English on me—which sometimes had us laughing—the camp's workday was coming to an end. Outside the windows, dusk was falling.

Assuring them that I was leaving town the next morning, eventually I was escorted to the gate without ever meeting the man in charge. Much to my relief, I headed to my hotel to get something to eat and attempt to sleep. As the sun rose the next morning, I headed out of town, certain that my departure was being closely monitored.

I tell this story as an example of confident humility. In this situation the soldiers held all the cards (and the guns). Needless to say, any arrogance on my part could have gotten me thrown into prison with little or no recourse. As a visitor to many foreign countries over the years, I had long since learned to be respectful of the people, culture, customs, and rules. But that particular experience ramped my awareness to new heights! That day I leaned deeply into presence, equanimity, strategic patience, and the keen knowing that in each moment I was in choice regarding how I presented myself. I was in choice with how I engaged with the soldiers. How at ease I was and how I could make them feel connected as human beings was up to me. That didn't negate the potential danger, but it did shape the way I was able to stay grounded and allow myself to have compassion for them, for me, for all of us in the situation. Let me just say, however, that I was more than happy to get back home safely to be able to get to talk about it!

The leadership imperative

Inherent in leadership is the implicit expectation that leaders have the answers. It is something leaders internalize and people in organizations or communities often demand—even while simultaneously saying they want a voice in decision-making. It's definitely complicated.

A leader's approach to advancing an organization, an initiative, a cause, cascades throughout the collective, shaping identity, setting the tone for decision-making processes, influencing risk tolerance and innovation, and shaping communication patterns. It influences hiring, elevates individuals to expanded levels of responsibility, affects stakeholder relationships, influences market perception, shapes customer interactions and has a direct impact on the bottom line.

Leaders demonstrating confident humility seek diverse perspectives, encourage transparency in decision making, and acknowledge uncertainty and their need to learn more. They're willing to change course when evidence suggests it's necessary. They nurture environments where team members feel safe admitting mistakes, asking for help, and sharing learning experiences, thus creating robust feedback mechanisms. These are key elements for building psychological safety.

From startups to large multi-national corporations, and other organizations fortunate enough and smart enough to foster confident humility in their leaders typically demonstrate higher innovation rates because risk-taking, experimentation and learning from failure are encouraged. There is better risk management because diverse perspectives and approaches are the norm. Trust is high, producing stronger team cohesion. And when teams see their work as more than transactional—when they have the long view—sustainable growth is more likely. Most of all, people want to be there because they feel valued in a culture where there is the understanding "We are human beings first, here to contribute, collaborate, and make a difference."

Nurturing confident humility

Confident humility requires intentional practice and self-reflection. Here are some suggestions for its development:

- **Periodically have a self-reflection session** to assess personal strengths and areas that challenge you. Which principles can help you strengthen those areas?
- **Find a trusted partner** you can share what you see in yourself, what you have learned in your own self-reflection and vice versa.
- **Seek feedback from trusted sources**: Create 3 or 4 questions that will provide you meaningful and relevant feedback about your strengths and weaknesses.

Ask somebody you trust to meet in person for a "personal feedback assessment" session. Give them your questions and ask them to consider these as focus for the meeting. You have the option of adding the following open-ended question: "Is there something else you would like me to know that could contribute to my success?" Offer to return the favor of giving feedback to them at another time.

- **Dissect your beliefs around fear of failure:** It's not the failure we fear, but the potential consequences (real or imagined), and the meaning we give it. Start with asking yourself things like "What's the worst that can happen? What meaning am I giving this? What is likely to happen? How do I know?"

- **Assess the risk/ benefit** with partners, leaders, stakeholders—make them part of the process. Which principles can strengthen your capacity for navigating these experiences?

- **Approach new situations with openness and a "beginner's mind"**—value the learning.

- **Know that successes and failures do not define you.** They are results of actions and decisions, tactics and strategies, all of which can be evaluated, re-created, learned from, or changed in subsequent endeavors. Remember this.

On an organizational level:

Do the following audit to determine if confident humility exists systemically in leadership, culture, decision-making practices, system development and team development:

- **Do leaders demonstrate openness to feedback?** Do they express gratitude to the messenger? Are mistakes treated as learning opportunities? What is the evidence of that? Is success celebrated? Is it on the individual, team, or organization level, or all of the above?

- **How are the leaders defining success?** For example, in addition to gaining market share, landing that new client, inventing the latest biotech gadget, do they (and you) celebrate the "success" of finding a glaring hole in a process or system that, when remedied, ultimately saves the organization money, time, reputation and customer relationships?

- **Does senior leadership practice confident humility?** This is a competency that needs to be supported with shared learning for it to work. CEO: have deep conversations with your senior team to understand confident humility and assess if or how it shows up. Decide as a team to adopt this as a tenet of your stewardship of the organization. Commit to growing and living this competency for a few months. Let people experience it, share what you've all learned. Repeat. After a few months others have observed this behavior naturally. Only then should you consider taking it broadly into the organization.

Behavior change by proclamation never works. Embody it first then support it into the organization.

- **Be curious about the decision-making practices** in the organization and in yourself. Provide tools to support different approaches (i.e. Discern when and where it can be most appropriate and effective, and implement structured devil's advocate processes).

- **Create formal feedback channels at all organizational levels** as a place for the "end-users" of a specific decision implementation to provide real-time reporting on how it's going. Don't assume no news is good news. Review and, if needed, adjust strategies based on evidence.

Conclusion

Confident humility is a fundamental approach to life that is, perhaps, one of the most challenging and rewarding paths one can undertake, requiring constant vigilance against the seductive pull of arrogance. But the end result becoming a more courageous, balanced, wise, and dependable human being is worth the journey.

Reflective questions:

1. Is there a situation you can recall where unexpectedly you were asked to take part in a process where you felt like a fish out of water? Over your head? Thinking *What am I doing here?* How comfortable were you with the uncertainty? What was your internal

reaction? What was your external reaction? What was the outcome?

2. Recall an important decision you had to make recently. Did you consider seeking input from others? What made you decide to do that or not do that? In retrospect, did your choice effect the outcome? What might this reveal about your current balance of confidence and humility?

3. Reflect on a recent failure or setback. How did your level of confidence affect the situation? What role did humility (or its absence) play in how you handled and learned from this experience?

4. Consider a complex situation you're currently facing. Describe the actions you will take to approach it with confident humility and the principles you will include to do this. Is this a different approach than you would usually take?

5. When interacting with others who hold different views or expertise, how do you balance confidence in your own knowledge with openness to their perspectives? What could you do to improve this balance?

PRINCIPLE #21

VISION 2.0: THE VISION QUEST OF THE SPIRIT

What lies behind you and what lies in front of you, pales in comparison to what lies inside of you.

~ Ralph Waldo Emerson

Throughout human history, the power of vision has served as a beacon, guiding individuals and civilizations toward their highest aspirations. From solitary vision quests to collective organizational futurizing, the need to see clearly what lies ahead—and to hold fast to that vision—has been fundamental to human achievement and transformation for thousands of years.

We examined this kind of vision at length in Principle #11 in Vision 1.0. Here, in this second-to-last exploration of adventure principles, I will venture onto more esoteric ground and try to explain Vision 2.0

Often, when talking about "obtaining a vision," people are referring to the Native American vision quest. Known by different names among various tribes, it represents one of humanity's most profound traditions for seeking personal vision and life purpose. The Australian Aboriginal walkabout is similar, as are the medicine walks of various South American tribes. All these practices share the common elements of seeking answers to life's problems, searching for a higher ideal to follow, and/or finding personal inspiration and direction in life through spending extended periods of time in solitude in nature, going into deep silence to listen for what is calling you.

Whether in traditional or modern contexts, to this day, these practices continue to offer powerful means for individuals to connect with deeper sources of wisdom in order to help clarify their life purpose and place in society. But this application of the vision quest is all about vision 1.0 and (usually) more personal discovery. It can involve others. It can be a call to more spiritual work and healing. It can be a call to leadership. It is *always* about personal change and evolution and can result in an enormous uprooting of past perceptions and focus. A vision quest can shake your life apart and force you to rebuild on new foundations. But the overarching purpose of vision 1.0 is ultimately pragmatic.

Vision 2.0—and a vision quest 2.0—on the other hand, is about entering into dimensions beyond the personal and the practical, seeking entry into the unknown to see what the Great Mystery of life itself has to say. Which, in some ways, is what adventurers do when they set out on a journey into unexplored regions. They know they can prepare in every way and still be unprepared when they encounter the unknown. Uncertainty is around the next bend, over the next hill, beyond the visible horizon, and in the cosmos. A state of wonder takes over and the deepest energy of awareness reveals a vulnerability, which if embraced and not feared can be a doorway into the mystery. And to be able to get a handle on the reality of this possibility, let's first take a look at something called Maslow's Hierarchy of Needs.

The human hierarchy of needs

Dr. Abraham Maslow was a professor of psychology at Brandeis University and Columbia University, and one of the founders of transpersonal psychology, an area of psychology that seeks to integrate the spiritual and transcendent human experiences within the framework of modern psychology.

Briefly, Maslow believed that humans evolve through five levels of consciousness. Each level builds upon its predecessors, requiring integration of all the experiences and awareness gathered from all the previous levels before a person moves to the next level of consciousness.[74] His Needs Hierarchy provides a very clear picture of human psycho-spiritual evolution:

MASLOW'S HIERARCHY OF NEEDS

TRANS-PERSONAL: identity beyond the personal self

SELF-ACTUALIZATION: highest self-expression personal creativity expressed

ESTEEM NEEDS: respect • admiration • self-pride • accomplishment — PSYCHOLOGICAL

BELONGING NEEDS: love • friendship • community

SAFETY NEEDS: security • housing • money — BASIC

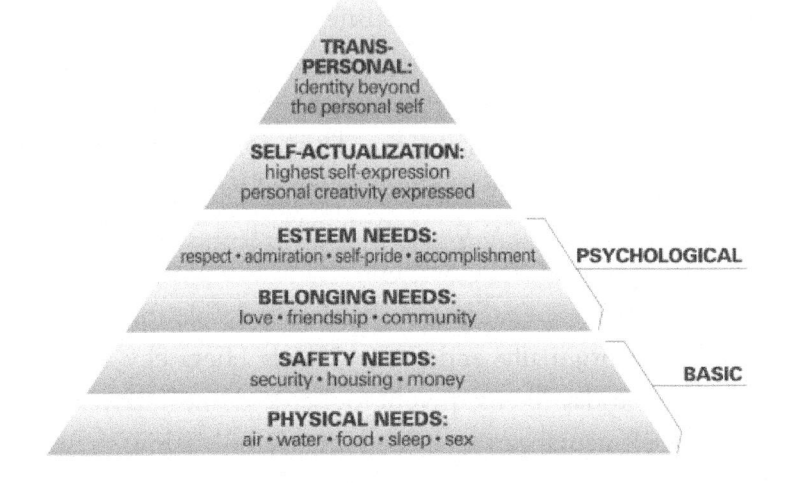

PHYSICAL NEEDS: air • water • food • sleep • sex

At the bottom of human needs are air, water, food, rest, sleep and a sexual, procreative outlet. After fundamental physical issues are handled, safety concerns arise. Having a mere roof overhead gives way to the desire for secure housing—a protected environment safe from future physical, mental and emotional harm—as well as a certain level of financial or bartering security to perpetuate these things.

If physiological and safety needs are met the next set of needs to show up is "belonging needs"—the desire to be part of a community and family and to have friends as a means of satisfying the human requirement for love, connection and nurturing. Once family and social networks have been created and *belonging* needs are satisfied, something called "esteem needs" quickly follow on the psychological horizon.

Being in a group, whether at work, socially or in a family, the ego develops the natural desire for recognition and respect. The need for self-esteem and the desire for a personal sense of accomplishment and meaningfulness arise. At this fourth level of consciousness, a growing interest in knowledge and beauty begins to develop, as well as a yearning for the fulfillment of such abstract concepts as freedom, justice and wisdom. Finally, the desire for a more fulfilling life on one's own terms evolves—a life of personal flowering and expression. This is the fifth level called "self-actualization," the point of development where the potential of the personal ego is expressed in the highest possible form.

Maslow originally ended the Needs Hierarchy at level five. Even today many psychologists and most laypersons perceive self-actualization as the pinnacle of Maslow's system as well as the highest possible level of human experience and expression. But later in life Maslow added a sixth level of human operation that transcended personal needs and strict ego-identification called the *transpersonal* level.[75]

> *"Self-actualization," the point of development where the potential of the personal ego is expressed in the highest possible form.*

You almost never see it in diagrams, but at this level of consciousness the personal ego has integrated all the previous levels and expanded self-actualization into an awareness of global and/or universal interconnection and a sense of self that extends *beyond* the personal to include humanity and life itself. The transpersonal level has tapped into the consciousness of the whole, or what various spiritual and philosophical traditions, including Eastern philosophies like Buddhism and Hinduism, as well as Western mysticism, call Unity Consciousness—the experience of transcending the individual self to experience a collective consciousness that binds all life together.

This is the realm of Vision 2.0.

As you can see from the diagram, vision 1.0 can be easily applied to the first five levels of Maslow's human needs hierarchy. But once you go past the level of personal wants and needs, the field explodes out of the known realm of human experience into the unknown. So, what, you might ask, is the point of venturing into this space? Why am I even talking about this? Well, this couldn't be a book about *adventure* principles without at least mentioning the greatest adventure of all: The mystery of the unseen and the yet-to-be-expressed potentials of human beings venturing into the collective consciousness of "the One," aka the realms of the divine.

Self-transcendence, as defined by Maslow in his later works, refers to the process by which individuals move beyond their own personal needs and self-fulfillment to connect with higher purposes, values, and goals outside of themselves. While self-actualization is focused on realizing one's personal potential, self-transcendence involves transcending the personal ego and identifying with something greater, such as the well-being of others, the environment, or a spiritual or religious belief system. This shift from self-centered goals to broader motivations marks a significant evolution in Maslow's hierarchy, highlighting the human capacity for growth beyond personal achievement.[76]

Buckminster Fuller once notably declared, "We are called to be architects of the future, not its victims. The challenge is to make the world work for 100% of humanity in the shortest possible time, with spontaneous cooperation, and without ecological damage or disadvantage of anyone."[77] This powerful statement encapsulates the proactive nature of vision and intention-setting. When we set clear intentions, we begin to architect our future rather than merely react to circumstances. And we can do this on more than just the mundane, pragmatic level of creating a nice life for ourselves here on planet earth.

Maslow demonstrates—as every successful adventurer and explorer demonstrates—that we must attend to the basics before anything else. And creating a nice, happy, fulfilling life for ourselves and our families is the foundation. But eventually there is an urging to experience *more*. What about creating a nice, happy, fulfilling life for everybody on the planet? How would that be possible? How do we create such a world? Who/what do we have to become to actualize this greater vision? Does this vision entice you? The itch to help create a better world? A desire for more? This is the calling to Vision 2.0. How we get there is unknown. But that should not deter us. Most certainly this new adventure starts with the intention "to architect" such a future. And we can at least start the process with the tools we've got. We can start by becoming the wisest person we can be. We can start by learning to embody the adventure principles laid out in this book. We can start by asking the question "How do we get there?" and then applying the vision quest protocols above.

And we don't have to find a shaman to help guide us or travel to a remote place and sit alone in the wilderness to do this. We can start by simply taking time out every day to go sit under a tree in a park or in a nearby open space. We can start by simply asking: "How do we get there? What can I do to help us get there? What lies beyond the known for me?" And then listen.

Maslow's adventure

I would be remiss if I didn't touch on an experience that a 30-year-old Maslow had in 1938 when he spent six weeks living with the Siksika Nation, a Blackfoot First Nation in southern Alberta, Canada. He intended to test the universality of his early sociological theory that social hierarchies are maintained by dominance of some people over others. But he didn't see the quest for dominance in Blackfoot society.

Instead, he discovered astounding levels of cooperation, minimal inequality, restorative justice, full bellies, and high levels of life satisfaction.

In Blackfoot culture, he noted, a person is treated with dignity from birth onwards, and tribal members spend their lives living up to the trust and space they are given to express their unique selves rather than having to spend their lives competing to make money, living up to external social roles and expectations. The tribe recognizes that every member is imbued with a spark of divinity, and the only social mandate is to "be the best they can be"—an inherently sacred quest everybody takes very seriously through education, prayer, rituals, ceremonies, individual experiences, and vision quests.

He estimated that 80 to 90 percent of the Blackfoot tribe experienced a quality of self-esteem that was only found in 5 to 10 percent of his own population. And the discovery led him to rethink his early social theories. When Maslow published his work a few years later, it was not about social hierarchies and dominance, it was about the personal development of the individual and what facilitated growth and what did not. From this work his famous Hierarchy of Needs was born, along with the concept of self-actualization as an advanced state of human consciousness that could only be arrived at after all personal needs were supported and experienced in a culture of caring and compassion and communal self-reliance.

Obviously, there is a lot to be learned from the Blackfoot Nation that could be good for humanity.

Conclusion

"Ask and ye shall receive" is probably one of the best-known sayings in the Bible because it is a great truth. When we ask, we set the quest in motion where vision serves as both compass and catalyst, guiding us toward desired futures while energizing the journey there. As architect Daniel Burnham advised, "Make no little plans; they have no magic to stir men's blood." It's going to take a little "magic" to turn this world around. But I know of no greater vision to hold or greater adventure to go on than to try to make it happen.

Reflective questions

1. Do you have an audacious thought or imagining of something that may seem impossible to achieve? What is it?

2. Seeing the impossible as possible is a matter of perspective. If you weren't arguing with yourself about what's not possible ... what could be possible?

3. Vision into the unknown seems paradoxical. How can you have a vision for something you can't name? Seems impossible, impractical, and like magical thinking. Hmmm...What if it's not? Do you feel comfortable opening the door to the unknown? What does it bring up inside? All responses are acceptable. How can there be a "right" response to the unknown?

PRINCIPLE # 22

TRANSCENDENCE AND TRANSFORMATION

"Your task is not to seek for love, but merely to seek and find all the barriers within yourself that you have built against it."

~ Jalāl al-Dīn Rumi

If you've taken to heart the preceding principles in this book and find yourself attracted to inner transformation, that is a wonderful thing. And if you have found value and inspiration in the preceding principles, that is all I could possibly hope for. But now, with this final principle (which I'm not sure is actually a "principle" or not), we face a mountain summit like no other.

Transformation can be defined as the process by which an individual moves beyond their conventional boundaries of self-understanding and worldly constraints to experience a profound shift in consciousness, perspective, and identity. It represents not merely incremental growth or improvement, but rather a fundamental reconstitution of being—a metamorphosis of the self that results in qualitatively different modes of perception, understanding, and engagement with reality. At the core of the definition of transformation is a significant change in form, structure, or character, often leading to a new state. The best, if hackneyed, example is the butterfly that starts out life as an unattractive lowly worm and ends up as a brilliant jeweled butterfly. Now *that* is transformation.

Transformation can happen intentionally and accidentally. You can focus your intention on living a transformative life and use specific approaches like meditation, yoga, qigong, therapy, and practices such as those outlined in this book, to create tremendous shifts in yourself over and over again. You can undergo an unexpected spiritual awakening triggered by various factors, including personal crises, transformative experiences, or even seemingly mundane conversations that lead to questioning and shifting your perspective on life, meaning, and purpose. You can be volunteering at a youth center and suddenly find yourself looking beyond your personal concerns with a heightened awareness of the importance of connection, deeper meaning, personal fulfillment and growth.

And then there is "transcendence," a word that can be traced through its etymology from the Latin prefix "trans" meaning "beyond" and the word "scandare," meaning "to climb." In my own life I've had transcendent experiences of peace, awe, gratitude, happiness, joy, and love that elevated me beyond my day-to-day consciousness. Being in nature does that for a lot of people, and I don't believe there is a minimum threshold for defining an experience as transcendent or transformative.

A situation may seem mundane, be inherently dramatic or exceptionally unique. It's transformative power lies in how it affects us, and it's strictly an individual thing. For example, participating in team-building organizational ropes courses, I've seen people climb the tallest tree and launch themselves into mid-air, trusting their harness and their team without a moment's hesitation. They had fun, but they didn't transcend or transform their limitations. On the other hand, the person terrified of heights who managed to shake, cry, and quiver their way up onto the third step of the tree ladder not four feet off the ground has definitely climbed beyond their limits.

As you can imagine, the concept of "climbing beyond" resonates deeply with most adventurers I know, myself included. And yet, in the long run, we can only climb so far. If we look back at Maslow's Hierarchy of Needs diagram, there are rungs we ascend mentally, emotionally, physically and spiritually all the way up through the transpersonal levels which go beyond the material and personal aspects of life, connecting us to a larger sense of existence and a connection with a higher power or a sense of unity with all things.

But then there is another kind of transcendence that even Maslow didn't have the nerve to talk about. A spiritual transcendence that, literally, takes us beyond our humanity. As you will see shortly, apparently there are no "steps toward" final transcendence, which is also referred to in Eastern spiritual philosophies as enlightenment. Much like the "something

> There are no "steps toward" final transcendence. It just "happens" when and if the time is right and nature, or God, or Source, or the intelligence of the quantum field deems it should happen.

else" we talked about in Principle 19 on creativity, intention might set the stage, but ultimate transcendence in the classic sense of transcending our human condition—aka enlightenment—just "happens" when and *if* the time is right and nature, or God, or Source, or the intelligence of the quantum field of Oneness deems it should happen.

Spiritual transcendence

In Christianity, the best and most central example of transformation and then final transcendence beyond the human is the life of Jesus Christ. The metamorphosis from Jesus of Nazareth, the carpenter's son, to Christ, the anointed one and embodiment of divine love, represents the archetypal pattern of spiritual transformation and then transcendence. The Gospel narratives trace this journey through baptism, temptation in the wilderness, transfiguration, crucifixion, and resurrection—each stage marking a deepening embodiment of divine consciousness.

Buddhism is the result of the transformation of Prince Siddhartha who abandoned his royal blood and privilege to seek liberation from human suffering, journeying through asceticism until he finds the Middle Path, eventually coming to his enlightenment beneath the Bodhi tree. At this point he transcended his humanity and became the Buddha—the

Awakened One. The next forty-five years the Buddha taught a systematic approach to transformation and ultimate transcendence/liberation from the human condition through the extinguishing of craving and the illusion of a separate self through direct experience beyond conceptual understanding.

In Hinduism, the concept of moksha—liberation from the cycle of rebirth and suffering—represents the ultimate transcendence involving the realization of one's true nature as eternal and identical with universal consciousness. Within Islam, the Sufi path may be the clearest tradition of transformation. Sufism describes a journey through successive stages and states of consciousness leading to the annihilation of the separate self and subsistence in God. This process involves the progressive refinement of the ego-self through practices of remembrance, contemplation, and love. The 13th-century poet Jalāl al-Dīn Rumi articulates this journey with great eloquence saying: "Your task is not to seek for love, but merely to seek and find all the barriers within yourself that you have built against it."

During my years practicing Tai Chi and learning about Taoism, I've seen how the key element of transformation is about being caught up in the embrace of the interconnectedness of all life and the universe. The Tao is the natural way of the universe when the illusion of separateness dissolves.

For the indigenous people of the Amazon rainforest, such as the Achuar and others, as well as the Quechua and other indigenous people of the Andes mountains, ecological consciousness is inseparable from their spirituality at the essence of who they are. They experience kinship with all beings and rather than transcending nature, they transcend the limited human perspective and cultural illusion of separation from nature.

Most spiritual traditions employ metaphors of death and rebirth, suggesting that true transcendence requires a kind of ego-death preceding the emergence of a more expansive identity. Virtually all recognize the importance of teachers or guides who have themselves undergone transformation.

A non-personal, non-experience experience

While working on this last principle, I discovered that the writer friend I talked about in Principle #19, Cate Montana, has written a book about the transcendence of human consciousness—aka enlightenment—based upon her own experience. She makes an important distinction about the topic this way, saying "Enlightenment isn't something you experience or attain because there's no 'you' around to experience or attain anything. There's just pure non-personal Isness." To explain what she means by that, she told me a great story about her "non-experience" of enlightenment which she describes in her book, *The E Word: Ego, Enlightenment & Other Essentials*.[78]

Basically, after about 20,000 hours of meditation, she found that her personal identity and the illusion of her humanity began to crack. She told me that the ego "I" naturally started falling away during meditation, making room for "non-dual awareness"—a blissful state of unity consciousness where the separate sense of self disappears, opening the door to an awareness of the much vaster ocean of consciousness. In some spiritual traditions this level of consciousness is referred to simply as "I AM."

As she persevered, one morning the non-dual state of consciousness persisted for a much longer period of time—three days in fact. She told me that during this time there was no "I" around. No personality to do anything "normal" with the information that was arriving through the senses—no normal "Cate" reactions or thoughts. As she put it, "There was no one home to judge or worry about anything." She described a holographic array of information containing all her lived experience as well as all that is in timeless eternity. She stressed that one single word tagged onto the "I AM" statement, such as "I am human," or "I am a woman" or "I am physical" was an expression of limited personal identity and ultimately an illusion.

However, after a few days of pure existence as boundless as the universe, the mind of "Cate" began to reform until she was, once again, human. "It was the most devastating, awful experience," she said. "Like taking forever and slamming it into a tiny dark closet and throwing away the key."

A much-changed person, it took her years to make sense of how she ended up understanding the enlightened mind while being unenlightened—stuck in a state of consciousness that contained both points of view: unity and duality. Eventually she realized the three-day "non-experience experience" had deposited her squarely in the transpersonal mindset psychologist Abraham Maslow talked about—the *transition state* between personal (ego) consciousness and the transcendent state of egoless enlightenment. The in-between stage of ego expansion (not ego inflation) where we are set free to be our divine human selves—a deeply interconnected, compassionate consciousness that can be developed that is quite literally incapable of cruelty, destruction and harm to others and totally capable of (in fact designed for) the task of helping create heaven on Earth.

The story that Cate told me (which I appreciate her giving me permission to share), is a modern corroboration of other spiritual stories from history about divine transcendence. It's consistent with stories I've heard from a very small number of people. It also aligns with a direct experience I had during a long wilderness solo journey—a very brief glimpse into the non-dual "all-that-is" or "I AM" consciousness. I'll write more about that in a future book. Meanwhile, I encourage you to read Cate's book, not just for her great story, but her other wisdom as well.

The ultimate adventure

The key point I want to make is this: Human beings are much more than what we currently perceive ourselves to be. As a universal concept across human cultures, transcendence speaks to a collective intuition that the world as commonly perceived represents only one level of reality, and that deeper, more fulfilling modes of existence await those willing to undertake the necessary journey.

When we consider the relationship between transformation, transcendence, and adventuring, we discover profound parallels. Both the inward journey of spiritual development and the outward journey of exploration share essential qualities: 1) Both require courage to venture into unknown territory, 2) both demand resilience in the face of challenges, and 3) both ultimately yield expanded perspectives that could not have been attained without leaving familiar shores. The spiritual adept scaling the heights of consciousness and the explorer traversing unmapped territories are engaged in fundamentally similar enterprises—they seek to expand the boundaries of known experience and return with wisdom that benefits themselves and others.

> **The ultimate adventure, it would seem, manifests in the journey toward enlightenment, wherein the soul's compass guides one through uncharted territories of consciousness.**

The ultimate adventure, it would seem, manifests in the journey toward enlightenment, wherein the soul's compass guides one through uncharted territories of consciousness. As the spiritual adventurer navigates life with authentic intention, hidden truths are unveiled—or, when necessary, interrogated—as new horizons of understanding emerge. The process unleashes what many traditions describe as the Inner Voice—that authentic expression of one's deepest nature that becomes increasingly accessible as layers of conditioning are shed through honest self-expression, reflection, and spiritual practice.

In examining transformation across spiritual traditions and contemporary frameworks like Maslow's hierarchy, we discover not only the diversity of approaches to this universal human potential but also striking commonalities that suggest fundamental truths about our nature and destiny as conscious beings. We stand at a pivotal moment in human evolution, facing unprecedented global challenges and opportunities. Transformation is imperative. Having a better understanding of the dynamics of transformation and the possibility of transcendence leaves us better equipped for navigating, and better yet, _creating_ our collective future.

The following are some ancient "tried and true" methods for getting beyond mental busyness and accessing more expanded states of consciousness.

Training our attention

Whether contemplative prayer, Buddhist zazen, Transcendental Meditation, muraqaba in Sufism, or secular mindfulness, it is important that we train our attention to remain present rather than habitually wandering. This sustained development of inner quietude and presence gradually reveals aspects of reality and self typically missed in the cacophony of ordinary awareness. Some practical approaches include:

Meditative Practices

- Beginning with brief daily periods of silent sitting, gradually extending duration
- Anchoring attention in sensory experience (breath, bodily sensations)
- Observing one's thoughts and emotions without trying to hold onto, track, or suppress them
- Alternating focused attention with open monitoring of whatever arises in awareness
- Incorporating awareness practices into daily activities—practicing presence and being "in the Now"
- Walking meditation - silently walk a labyrinth or other special place, feel your body relax with each step

- Other moving meditations - tai chi and qigong are two of my favorites

This cultivation of awareness aligns with Maslow's observation that self-transcenders exhibit "an increased tendency to perceive the world as a unity." Enhanced awareness reveals connections and patterns typically fragmented by selective attention.

Transformative Practices

These often involve choosing challenges that stretch one's capacities. Vision quests, retreats, fasting, pilgrimages, and service commitments all involve encountering limitations and moving beyond comfort zones. These practices reflect recognition that transformation and transcendence require facing aspects of reality we typically avoid. Practical approaches include:

- **Developing the capacity to stay present with uncomfortable emotions** without immediate reaction. To transform something we have to first recognize and then admit it's existence. Uncomfortable emotions turn us into great escape artists, leaning into the excuse that we are "too busy" to deal with that stuff. In reality, we are too uncomfortable to feel the uncomfortable emotion. We have to learn to get comfortable with discomfort. If we can do that, if we can acknowledge it and own it, we can do something with it. So, embrace your *dis*comfort zones so they can teach you what you need to learn. Only then can you release what owns you and transform the uncomfortable emotion into breathing space. Ahh...

- **Undertaking periodic fasts from food, media, or habitual comforts.** Often there is a sharpening of the senses or clarity that emerges following these fasts. (Be smart about this. Speak with your health provider to assess if or what type of fasting is for you).

- **Setting challenging service commitments that benefit others.** Shifting our time and attention to "tending to another" has a way of feeding our spirit and igniting our compassion, which may have been lying dormant for some time.

- **Engaging in wilderness experiences** that reduce reliance on technological buffers or anything that takes your attention away from this moment in this place—right here, right now. That means no books, no journals, no projects to keep you busy. (Unless you're repairing the hole in your tent!) The purpose is to remove any barrier between you and the nature place that immerses you. When you let all of the distractions fall away, you find space in your being to expand awareness into the infinite. Some pretty magical experiences have happened for me out on solo journeys. No psychoactive or hallucinatory substances involved, just connection with all that is.

- **Cultivation of gratitude through formal or informal practices.** We have talked a lot about this throughout the book, and there are many practices enumerated for you to utilize. Right in this moment as you are reading these words, simply ask yourself: "What am I grateful for today?"

- **Practicing difficult conversations with full presence rather than habitual defensiveness.** The hardest part of difficult conversations is to actually stay in the conversation and out of the chattering narrative in your head that is keeping you from full presence. You can't be fully present if you're attached to wanting to be right, or you're busy thinking of your responses while the other person is still talking. And there can be no constructive outcomes if you can't let yourself think there could be a solution you haven't imagined yet. Or that the other person might be the one to come up with it. I could go on, but you see what I am saying. *To transform a situation, you can only transform yourself.* If you can start with that, wisdom has a fighting chance.

These practices develop what Maslow called the "meta-motivation characteristics of transcenders"—motivation not by deficiency needs but by growth values that may involve temporary discomfort for greater understanding.

Immersion in nature

Indigenous cultures emphasize relationship with the natural world as a path to transformation for good reason. Regular immersion in nature is one of the easiest, most pleasant pathways to absorbing pure love and grounding into our deepest, most spiritual "self." The term forest bathing emerged in Japan in the 1980's. It had dual purpose—to offer an eco-antidote to tech-boom burnout and to inspire people to reconnect with and protect the country's forests. Research began in the 1990s, and no surprise, *shinrin-yoku,* aka forest bathing has been clinically proven to reduce stress, mitigate PTSD, lower blood pressure, alleviate depression, and improve mental health.[79]

- Nature is all around us. Even in the densest "concrete jungle" of a city, you can find nature if you look for it - a tree to sit under, a random garden, the weed that that found the crack in the sidewalk to reach for the sun; look up and meditate on the passing clouds in the sky. Be intentional and take 15 minutes a day, *without your phone,* to look - and marvel at what you see.

- Practice shinrin-yoku (forest bathing). Go to local parks, Tea Gardens, Botanical Gardens, any of the National or State Parks, or open space that calls you. Slow your mind and your pace. Pay attention to your surroundings using all of your senses. Stay present to your experience of connecting to nature.

- Experience a sweat lodge. The sweat lodge is a sacred ceremonial practice for prayer, purification, and spiritual cleansing. Learn about individual sweat lodge communities and their practices before choosing to do this.

- Join a hiking club or some other outdoor group—something that gets you out there doing something you like.

- Go camping. (And don't feed the bears!)

Human Connection

Being with others is surprisingly necessary for personal transformation. As the old saying goes, "We're wounded in relationship and thus we must heal in relationship." Though transformation may appear a solitary process, most traditions emphasize the importance of community in supporting transformation. Buddhist sangha, Christian communion, indigenous tribal ceremonies, and other collective practices recognize that transformation rarely occurs in isolation.

Mindfulness practices, contemplative inquiry, somatic awareness approaches, and other methodologies for consciousness development have reached populations previously without access, creating potential for widespread cultivation of transformational awareness. Social experiments in collaborative governance, regenerative economics, and sustainable community demonstrate practical applications of transformational awareness in collective organizations.

Support your personal growth:

- Practice service to others as context for transcending self-concern.
- Practice honest communication that transcends social masks.
- Seek out and participate in communities with shared commitment to personal growth.

As Catholic priest, cultural historian, and ecotheologian Thomas Berry has pointed out, moving humanity beyond separate, egoic identity toward recognition of its embeddedness in larger living systems is the "Great Work" of our times.[80] Transformative practices from all traditions will be needed to help us transition from a consciousness of competitive, self-centered, exploitative living into a higher consciousness characterized by peace, connection, and mutual benefit and support.

Bottom line, technological solutions that don't reflect a profound advancement in human consciousness cannot take humanity where we want and need to go. Fortunately, growing numbers of individuals across diverse backgrounds are reporting spontaneous experiences of expanded consciousness characterized by profound interconnection, compassion beyond conventional boundaries, and perception of sacred dimensions to reality. Far from representing abstract or esoteric concerns, transformational information and practices are emerging as central to both individual fulfillment and collective flourishing at this pivotal historic moment in human evolution.

Reflective questions

Ask yourself:

1. What challenging experiences have led to significant personal transformation in my life, and what did I learn from them?

2. To what extent am I willing to embrace discomfort and challenge in the pursuit of personal growth, and what does this willingness reveal about my values and priorities?

3. What are some of the barriers, both internal and external, that hinder my personal transformation and how can I overcome them?

4. How do my relationships support or hinder my journey of transformation?

5. How can I intentionally incorporate challenges into my life to foster personal transformation and growth?

6. In what ways can this principle of transformation be applied to my work or career, and how might this foster greater creativity, collaboration, and purpose?

CONCLUDING THOUGHTS

MAKING ADVENTURE PRINCIPLES WORK FOR YOU

Throughout this book, we've explored the powerful connection between an adventure mindset and success—success not only in terms of personal development and the ability to navigate a world of rapid change and increasing chaos, but success in terms of helping set the creation of a transformed world into motion. Now we'll shift our focus from understanding these principles to putting them into action.

The principles we've covered, from embracing impermanence to cultivating confident humility, offer a powerful framework for navigating a complex world. However, their true value lies not in intellectual understanding but in practical application. To bridge this gap between concept and practice, I've included reflective questions at the end of most principles that you've already seen and (hopefully) contemplated. If you skipped through these questions to get to the end, now is a good time to start practicing Principle #14, Strategic Patience, and go back and start addressing them, principle by principle. In addition, you may also want to consider the following:

Adventure Integration Process

- **Self-assessment:** Begin by honestly evaluating your current mindset and behaviors around adventure. Which of the 22 Principles do you already embody? Where do you have the greatest opportunity for growth? This self-reflection lays the foundation for targeted development.

- **Prioritization:** You don't have to tackle all 22 principles at once. Choose two or three that resonate most strongly or address your most pressing challenges. Focus your initial efforts on mastering these, building momentum for further integration.

- **Action planning:** Go back and contemplate the answers you gave to the questions on the principles you select. (Or answer them for the first time.) Based on your answers and insights, create a specific action plan for integrating your chosen principle(s) into your daily life. This might involve setting reminders, creating new habits, or seeking out opportunities to practice the principle(s) in specific situations.

- **Mindful practice:** As you implement your action plan, pay close attention to your thoughts, feelings, and behaviors. Notice how applying each principle affects your decision-making, relationships, and overall well-being.

- **Adaptation and refinement:** The adventure mindset is not about rigid adherence to rules but about flexible adaptation to changing circumstances. As you practice, be willing to adjust your approach, experiment with new techniques, and refine your understanding of the principles.

- **Expansion:** Once you feel comfortable with one or two principles, expand your focus to include others. Gradually weave more adventure-tested tools into your mindset and behaviors, creating a resilient foundation for navigating life's ongoing challenges.

Sustainable change comes through consistent habits. In the process of turning adventure principles into daily practices you might want to start each day by asking, "What adventure am I choosing today?" Or perhaps it suits you better to end each day by documenting one way you stepped out of your comfort zone, one lesson learned, one insight gained, etc. The point being to link new adventure-minded behaviors to existing habits and routines.

Work with others

As part of understanding how adventure principles can be useful in your life, it is instructive to look around and see others who are successfully implementing these ideas. One obvious way to do this is to work with other like-minded people on implementing adventure principles. Also, see if you can identify others putting these principles into action—public figures, business leaders navigating disruptive markets, educators fostering student resilience, community organizers building social change movements—people transforming challenges into opportunities and creating sustainable success. By watching others, you can gain insights into how to bring these principles to life for yourself. Surround yourself with people who support your growth and values. Also, consider joining or forming an adventure mastermind group and/or mentoring others beginning their adventure journey. Create opportunities for others to safely expand their comfort zones. Share your adventure stories and lessons learned with family, friends, and co-workers. You don't know what you'll inspire in them and vice versa.

Adventure Perspective Framework

In my own life, I've integrated these principles in both my personal and professional journey. One of the core systems I use is an **Adventure Perspective Framework** that includes:

- **Daily exploration**: Every day, I aim to step outside my comfort zone. Whether it's learning a new skill, taking on a difficult conversation, or tackling a personal project, I use the opportunity to explore what I don't know.

- **The adventure circle**: I work to surround myself with a community of fellow adventurers—those who push me, inspire me, and hold me accountable. These people are crucial for maintaining my momentum and staying grounded.

- **Quarterly reflection and reset**: About every three months I take a "mini-expedition" to get out in nature and reflect on and review where I am in my life journey. This helps me recoup, rebalance, recalibrate and determine if my goals still align with my deeper purpose.

A lifelong practice

As we conclude our exploration of the adventure mindset, it's important to remember that this is not a destination but an ongoing journey. The world around us will continue to change, presenting new challenges and opportunities for growth. The key is to embrace this constant evolution with curiosity, courage, and a willingness to adapt.

Just as professional adventurers continue to hone their skills and seek out new challenges, we too must cultivate a lifelong practice of embracing the adventure mindset. This involves continuous learning and staying curious, seeking new experiences, and staying open to different perspectives. The more we learn, the better equipped we are to adapt to change, navigate uncertainty, and move toward creating our collective future in a transformed world.

Regularly take time to reflect on your experiences, identify areas for growth, and refine your approach to navigating challenges. **And take care of yourself.** Schedule regular "adventure audits" to get out in nature, restore your being, assess your growth, and set new challenges.

Remember, the world needs more people willing to embrace uncertainty, who find opportunity in challenge, and approach life with the heart of an adventurer. Start small. Every great adventure begins with just a single step. And you've already taken a big one by studying the Adventure

Mindset principles in this book. The only question that remains is: What adventure will you choose?

In the end, life itself is the greatest adventure of all. The adventure is yours. Step forward and thrive.

ACKNOWLEDGEMENTS

My deep gratitude to so many people who helped me put this book together as well as those who have inspired me along the way.

My wife Cheryl, who has been my best friend and adventure partner and great love of my life for over four decades. My brother Lee, who taught me finer points of mountain climbing, and my brother Todd, who taught me how to ride freight trains. Thank you to my sister Nancy, who showed me and others the adventure of living in other cultures. Thanks as well to my cousins, nieces, nephews, siblings-in-law, and all my other relatives with whom I continue to learn so much about love and life every day.

I also want to thank those who helped me learn about writing and publishing, including Raymond Aaron, who graciously shared his expertise in his excellent publishing workshop; the classes at Stanford led by Tiffany Hawk and others; my excellent editor Cate Montana, a fellow adventurer and author coach; the team at Hasmark—Judy, Ana-Maria, Jenn, Anne, and others who helped me through the steps of the publishing process.

Thanks also to all the teachers in my life, mentors and wise people who I've been blessed to have learned so much from, including: John P. Milton, founder of the Way of Nature, who has been a teacher and friend for more than three decades; Roy Bonney, an "old soul" who has been an important friend, healer, and mentor; Marie Diamond, a longtime friend and advisor; Darren Weissman, a friend, mentor and healer; Blaine Bartlett, a longtime friend who has graciously shared his wisdom; Stewart Emery, one of the fathers of the Human Potential Movement; Ivan Misner, founder of BNI, Lynne Twist, founder of Pachamama Alliance; as well as many others at educational institutions like Stanford, the University of Washington, University of New Hampshire.

A special mention to the Oregon Outdoor Program at the University of Oregon where I got to meet many kindred adventurers, including my adventure mates on the American Himalayan White Water Expedition of 1981 which accomplished the first successful descent of the Karnali River in Nepal.

Thank you to Outward Bound, the Mountaineers, the Way of Nature, and various other community and spiritual organizations that I've been fortunate to be welcomed into over the years. Thank you to the leaders of organizations I've learned so much from who hired me and mentored me along the way. Thank you to colleagues at non-profit and community organizations I've been involved with, including Rotary clubs in Palo Alto, San Francisco, Seattle, Tacoma, and elsewhere, the YMCA, Canopy, Emergency Food Network, LLS, Best Buddies, and others. Thank you to the many people at various professional organizations, including the Transformational Leadership Council, the ESOP Association, the NCEO, and other organizations that help advance knowledge in key areas.

Many thanks to people at those organizations and elsewhere who have inspired me. There are too many to name all of them, however here is a partial list:

> Jack Canfield, John Gray, Ken Honda, Deepak Chopra, Eric Edmeades, Roxanne Emmerich, Buckminster Fuller, Barnet Bain, Pete Bissonette, Paul Scheele, Ray

Acknowledgements

Blanchard, Rinaldo Brutoco, Dawson Church, Cherie Clark, Doria Cordova, Steve D'Annunzio, Bobbi DePorter, Steve Farber, Lisa Garr, Gabriel Nossovitch, Paul Scheele, Dawa Phillips, Lisa Nichols, Marci Shimoff, Carl Studna, Cynthia James, Kute Blackson, Kian Gohar, Kirsty Maynor, Patty Aubery, Ocean Robbins, Chunyi Lin, Claire Zammit, Craig Hamilton, Sally Jewell, Lise Janelle, Ken Wilcox, Don Arnoudse, Vazken Kalayjian, Vishen Lakhiani, Ben Boyer, John Cadeddu, Peter Chung, Jeff Clavier, Andy McLoughlin, Peter Hebert, Lila Ibrahim, Shawn Carolan, Carolin Funk, Dennis Jarosch, Andrew Chen, Christy Chin, Eric Chin, Matt Bigge, Murat Bicer, Naval Ravikant, Hemant Taneja, Pete Solvik, Greg Gretsch, Seth Godin, Chris Hsu, Chris Basso, Jeff Bird, Mike Speiser, Dave Sweet, Jim White, Bill Younger, Greg Sands, Andy Sheehan, Ron Chang, David Ron, Debra Dunn, Randy Komisar, Reid Hoffman, Jose Suarez, Noah Knauf, Sam Horn, Scott deMoulin, Shawn Conway, Tim Draper, Andy Tang, Christine Tsai, Hans Tung, Paul Vronsky, Tabreez Verjee, Bob Komin, Jim Kwik, Glenn Solomon, Peter Blackwood, Dave Armstrong, Michael Anderson, Vijay Pande, Jamie McGurk, Dave Mount, Brook Porter, Ben Kortlang, Dan Oros, Josh Stein, Mark Siegel, Saar Gur, Josh McFarland, Greg Goldfarb, Alex Kurland, Ronjon Nag, Ravi Narula, Vivian Glyck, Mike Koenigs, Mike Rayburn, Mike Zappert, Shelly Lefkoe, Ken Druck, Richard Strozzi-Heckler, Debra Poneman, Joan Emery, Arielle Ford, Brian Arthur, Martin Rutte, Bob Burgess, Greg Welch, Michelle Blackburn, Doug Canterbury-Counts, Nikole Kadel, Bill Smith, Maria Bailey, Zita Xavier, Steve Craven, Bud Wilson,

Mike Dooley, Anita Sanchez, Betty Spruill, Guillermo Paz, Sue Morter, Zen DeBrucke, Peggy Cappy, Andres Portillo, Cynthia Kersey, Anat Baniel, Sadhvi Saraswati, Christine Hibbard")

Thanks as well to so many of the adventurers whose thought leadership I've relied on as I developed the ideas in this book, including: Richard Branson, Liv Arnesen, Ann Bancroft, Yvon Chouinard, Reinhold Messner, Junko Tabei, Ed Viesturs, Ed Birnbaum, Erik Weihenmayer, Alex Honnold, Sarah Marquis, Diana Nyad, Wangari Maathai, Jessica Meir, Brené Brown, Meg Wheatley, Jim Collins, Eckhart Tolle, Peter Senge, Otto Scharmer, Joe Jaworski, Betty Sue Flowers, Jon Kabat-Zinn, Roz Savage, Dr. Ihaleakala Hew Len, Joe Vitale, Adam Grant, Ray Dalio, Eric Brymer, and Paula Reid.

And finally, **thank you** to those of you who have bought this book. May you find it worthwhile and helpful to your life and the adventures ahead!

ABOUT THE AUTHOR

Mark Stevenson is an accomplished adventurer and business leader who applies the wisdom of exploration and adventure to help individuals and organizations succeed in volatile markets and environments of rapid change. He believes this mindset enhances the ability to lead innovation by thinking big while looking to reduce risk to attain greater rewards.

Mark's adventurous background includes being part of the first successful descent of Nepal's remote Karnali River, trekking through deserts and rainforests, scaling peaks, riding freight trains, and engaging diverse indigenous cultures. His experience working in outdoor experiential education, including Outward Bound, has taught him that certain success principles apply equally to unexpected storms on a glacier or market disruptions and economic downturns.

His new book, *Adventure Mindset: 22 Principles for Growing and Thriving Amidst Chaos and Change,* translates lessons from navigating uncertainty in the wild into practical strategies for developing resilience and leadership skills. The book's wisdom, drawn from Mark's own journeys and other successful adventurers, as well as ancient wisdom traditions, reveals how to optimize human potential—mind, body, heart, and spirit—in the face of challenges, uncertainty, and chaos. This collected wisdom will guide readers toward personal growth, increased business acumen, healthier relationships, and a deeper connection with nature.

NOTES

[1] The concept of VUCA has been around since the 1980s, popularized by Warren Bennis & Burt Nanus who defined it as Volatility; Uncertainty, Complexity; Ambiguity. More recently it has been re-addressed and updated as VUCA Prime in 2007 by Bob Johannsen at the Institute of the Future as Vision, Understanding, Clarity, Adaptability. And Johannsen's colleague at the Institute of the Future Jamais Caisco, has introduced BANI: Brittle, Anxious, Non-Linear, Incomprehensible. Other related acronyms in use include TUNA, from Oxford University: Turbulent, Uncertain, Novel, Ambiguous. Also, RUPT, from the Center for Creative Leadership (ccl.org) has both negative connotation: Rapid, Unpredictable, Paradoxical, Tangled; AND positive: Reality, Understanding, Possibilities, Transparency. See https://www.vuca-world.org for more on this.

[2] Reid, Paula, and Eric Brymer. *Adventure Psychology: Going Knowingly into the Unknown* (Routledge Research in Health, Nature and the Environment). 2022. Kindle Edition.

[3] Milton, John P. *Sky Above Earth Below: Spiritual Practice in Nature.* Sentient Publications. 2006.

[4] Sealth, Chief. *Statement on Surrendering Tribal Lands to Isaac Stevens, Governor of Washington Territory in 1855.* WikiQuote. www.en.wikiquote.org/wiki/Chief_Seattle. Accessed June 2025.

5. Lorenz, Edward. *The Essence of Chaos*. University of Washington Press. 1995.
6. Messner, Reinhold. *Everest: Expedition to the Ultimate*. Mountaineers Books. 1999.
7. Brown, Brené. *Dare to Lead: Brave Work. Tough Conversations. Whole Hearts*. Random House. 2018.
8. Levitt, Steven and Stephen Dubner. *Think Like a Freak*. William Morrow. 2015.
9. Aurelius, Marcus. Meditations. Originally written in 180 AD. Edition of Meditations cited is the translation by Martin Hammond. Penguin Books. 2006. Also note: it was written in Greek without intention of publication by the only Roman emperor known to have also been a philosopher. The Meditations of Marcus Aurelius offer a remarkable series of challenging spiritual reflections and exercises developed as the emperor struggled to understand himself, make sense of the universe, provide personal consolation and encouragement, is a timeless work of philosophy that has been consulted and admired by statesmen, thinkers and readers throughout the centuries.
10. Frankl, Viktor. *Man's Search for Meaning*. Beacon Press. 2006.
11. Wilcox, Ken. *Leading Through Culture: How Real Leaders Create Cultures That Motivate People to Achieve Great Things*. Waterside Productions. 2020.
12. Aristotle, *Nicomachean Ethics*. Originally written 350 BCE. Editions of Nicomachean Ethics that were consulted include the translation by Bartlett, Robert, and Susan Collins. University of Chicago Press 2011, and Reeve, CDC Hackett, 2014
13. Brown, Donald. *Human Universals*. Temple Univ Press. 1991.
14. Dalai Lama XIV, *Ethics for the New Millennium*. Riverhead Books. 2001.

15 Scott, James M. *Fridtjof Nansen*. Heron Books. 1971.

16 Wheatley, Margaret J. *Leadership and the New Science: Discovering Order in a Chaotic World*. Berrett-Koehler Publishers. 2006. (First published 1992)

17 Collins, Jim. *Good To Great: Why Some Companies Make the Leap and Others Don't*. Harper Business. 2001

18 Simon, Herbert Alexander. *Reason in Human Affairs*. Stanford University Press. 1983.

19 Arthur, W. Brian. *Complexity and the Economy*. Oxford University Press. 2014.

20 Farmer, J. Doyne, *Making Sense of Chaos: A Better Economics for a Better World*. Yale University Press. 2024.

21 Worsley, Frank Arthur. *Shackleton's Boat Journey*. W. W. Norton & Company. 1998.

22 Alexander, Caroline. *The Endurance: Shackleton's Legendary Antarctic Expedition*. Knopf. 1998.

23 Lansing, Alfred. *Endurance: Shackleton's Incredible Voyage*. Basic Books. 2015.

24 Morrell, Margot, and Stephanie Capparell. *Shackleton's Way: Leadership Lessons from the Great Antarctic Explorer*. Penguin Books. 2002

25 Worsley, Frank. *Endurance; An Epic of Polar Adventure*. P. Allan & Co. 1931.

26 Ostrom, Elinor. *Governing the Commons: The Evolution of Institutions for Collective Action*. Cambridge University Press. 1990. and Ostrom, Elinor, et.al. *Working Together: Collective Action, the Commons, and Multiple Methods in Practice*. Princeton University Press. 2010.

[27] Versions of this have been said by many people including David Bohm and Dale Carnegie, however one of the most well-known sources of this is Stephen Covey in: Covey, Stephen. *The 7 Habits of Highly Effective People: Powerful Lessons in Personal Change*. Free Press. 1989.

[28] Gurdjieff, George Ivanovich. *Meetings with Remarkable Men*. Dutton. 1963.

[29] Bennett, John G. *An Introduction to Gurdjieff: Is There "Life" on Earth?* Stonehill Publishing Company. 1973.

[30] Tolle, Eckhart. www.eckharttolle.com. Accessed June 2025

[31] Kagge, Erling. *Silence: In the Age of Noise*. Penguin. 2017.

[32] Senge, Peter, C. Otto Scharmer, Joseph Jaworski, and Betty Sue Flowers. *Presence: Human Purpose and the Field of the Future*. Crown Currency. 2004.

[33] Milton, John P. *The Way of Nature*. www.wayofnature.com. Most recent access June 2025.

[34] Rinpoche, Ahiranta, et.al. *Ataraxia: The Freedom of a Calm Mind*. Self-Help Books. 2025

[35] Considerable mindfulness research continues to emerge and be published in the Journal of Neuroscience and other neuroscience journals. Among those that were consulted are these:

Lutz, Antoine, Helen Slagter, Nancy Rawlings, et.al. *Mental Training Enhances Attentional Stability: Neural and Behavioral Evidence*. Journal of Neuroscience. 2009 and Hölzel, BK. et al. *Mindfulness Practice Leads to Increases in Regional Brain Gray Matter Density*. Psychiatry Research: Neuroimaging. 2011.

[36] Kabat-Zinn, Jon. *Wherever You Go, There You Are: Mindfulness Meditation in Everyday Life*. Hyperion 1994. Other notable

books by Jon Kabat-Zinn on meditation and the elusive art of living fully in each moment as it unfolds, include: *Coming to Our Senses: Healing Ourselves and the World Through Mindfulness*. Hachette Books 2006, and *Full Catastrophe Living*. Random House 2007.

[37] Sullenberger, Chesley B. and Jeffrey Zaslow. *Highest Duty: My Search for What Really Matters*. William Morrow. 2009.

[38] This is attributed to Lucius Annaeus Seneca (c. 4 BC – A.D. 65), often known simply as Seneca, or Seneca the Younger, who was a Roman philosopher, statesman, dramatist, and humorist. Many of his writings can be found in the compilation: *Seneca's Morals of a Happy Life, Benefits, Anger and Clemency* (various translations and versions in public domain).

[39] Savage, Roz. *Rowing the Atlantic: Lessons Learned on the Open Ocean*. Simon & Schuster. 2009.

[40] Greenleaf, Robert K. *Servant Leadership: A Journey into the Nature of Legitimate Power and Greatness*. Paulist Press. 1977.

[41] Vitale, Joe, and Dr. Ihaleakala Hew Len. *Zero Limits: The Secret Hawaiian System for Wealth, Health, Peace, and More*. Wiley. 2008.

[42] Stone, William Clement. *The Success System that Never Fails*. Prentice-Hall. 1962.

[43] Tzu, Lao. (Translation by Stephen Mitchell). *Tao Te Ching* (New English Version). Harper Perennial 2006

[44] Turney, Chris. *1912: The Year the World Discovered Antarctica*. Counterpoint. 2012.

[45] Ballard, Robert D. *The Discovery of the Titanic*. Warner/Madison. 1988.

46 Mansfield, Victor. *Synchronicity, Science, and Soulmaking: Understanding Jungian Synchronicity Through Physics, Buddhism, and Philosophy.* Open Court. 1998.

47 Alastair Humphreys is an accomplished adventurer, author, and speaker with an excellent perspective on living adventurously. More information can be found at his website: www.alastairhumphreys.com

48 Watson, Jessica. *True Spirit: The True Story of a 16-Year-Old Australian Who Sailed Solo, Nonstop, and Unassisted Around the World.* Atria Books. 2010.

49 Brezsny, Rob. *Pronoia Is the Antidote for Paranoia.* North Atlantic Books. 2009.

50 Covey, Stephen R. *The 7 Habits of Highly Effective People: 30th Anniversary Edition.* Simon & Schuster. 2020.

51 Dalai Lama. *Beyond Religion: Ethics for a Whole World.* HarperOne. 2012.

52 Howard, Jane. *Margaret Mead: A Life.* Simon & Schuster. 1989.

53 Goodall, Jane, et.al. *The Book of Hope: A Survival Guide for Trying Times.* Celadon Books. 2021. See also the Jane Goodall Institute at: www.janegoodall.org

54 Cialdini, Robert B., *Influence, New and Expanded: The Psychology of Persuasion.* Harper Business 2021.

55 Grant, Adam. *Give and Take: Why Helping Others Drives Our Success.* Penguin Books. 2014.

56 Wallach, Janet. *Desert Queen: The Extraordinary Life of Gertrude Bell: Adventurer, Adviser to Kings, Ally of Lawrence of Arabia.* Anchor. 2005.

57 Zak, PJ, et.al. *Oxytocin Increases Generosity In Humans.* PLoS One. 2007.

58. McLean, Bethany and Peter Elkind. *The Smartest Guys in the Room: The Amazing Rise and Scandalous Fall of Enron.* Portfolio. 2013.

59. Arnesen, Liv, Ann Bancroft. *No Horizon Is So Far: Two Women and Their Historic Journey Across Antarctica.* Univ of Minnesota Press. 2019.

60. Elkington, John and Jochen Zeitz. *The Breakthrough Challenge: 10 Ways to Connect Today's Profits with Tomorrow's Bottom Line.* Jossey-Bass. 2014.

61. Elkington, John. *25 Years Ago I Coined the Phrase "Triple Bottom Line." Here's Why It's Time to Rethink It.* Harvard Business Review. 2018.

62. Elkington, John. *Green Swans: The Coming Boom in Regenerative Capitalism.* Fast Company Press. 2020.

63. Aesop. Olivia Temple (Translator). The Complete Fables. Penguin 2003

64. Tabei, Junko. *Honouring High Places: The Mountain Life of Junko Tabei.* Rocky Mountain Books. 2017.

65. Hutchinson, Gillian. S*ir John Franklin's Erebus and Terror Expedition: Lost and Found.* Adlard Coles. 2017.

66. Ward, William Arthur. *Think It Over: From The Writings of William Arthur Ward.* Fort Worth Star-Telegram. 1985

67. Isaacson, Walter. *Leonardo da Vinci.* Simon & Schuster. 2018.

68. Nickerson R. S., et.al. *The Teaching of Thinking.* Routledge. 2014.

69. Drucker, Peter F. *The Effective Executive: The Definitive Guide to Getting the Right Things Done.* Harper Business. 2006.

70. Dalio, Ray. *Principles: Life and Work.* Simon & Schuster. 2017.

71   Goodwin, Doris Kearns. *Team of Rivals: The Political Genius of Abraham Lincoln*. Simon & Schuster. 2006.

72   Branson, Richard. *Losing My Virginity: How I Survived, Had Fun, and Made a Fortune Doing Business My Way*. Crown Currency. 2011. See also: MacGregor, JR. *Richard Branson: The Force Behind Virgin: Insight and Analysis into the Life and Successes of Sir Richard Branson*. CAC Publishing. 2018.

73   Viesturs, Ed, and David Roberts. *No Shortcuts to the Top: Climbing the World's 14 Highest Peaks*. Broadway Books. 2006.

74   Maslow, Abraham H. *Hierarchy of Needs: A Theory of Human Motivation*. Psychology Classics. 2013.

75   Maslow, Abraham Harold. *Toward a Psychology of Being*. John Wiley & Sons. 1998.

76   Koltko-Rivera, ME. *Rediscovering the Later Version of Maslow's Hierarchy of Needs: Self-Transcendence and Opportunities for Theory, Research, and Unification*. Review of General Psychology. 2006.

77   Sieden, Steven. *A Fuller View: Buckminster Fuller's Vision of Hope and Abundance for All*. Divine Arts. 2012.

78   Montana, Cate. *The E-Word: Ego, Enlightenment & Other Essentials*. Atria/Enliven Books. 2017.

79   Fitzgerald, Sunny. *The Secret to Mindful Travel? A Walk in the Woods*. National Geographic website. 2019 www.nationalgeographic.com/travel/article/forest-bathing-nature-walk-health. Accessed June 2025

80   Berry, Thomas. *The Great Work: Our Way into the Future*. Crown. 2000.

INDEX

A

Acceptance
  of change, 11, 19, 20, 95
  of impermanence, 11, 18-20, 97
  of interconnectedness, 11, 14, 18-20
  of responsibility, 44, 131
Accountability
  as foundation of potential, 131-140
  and community, 138
  and integrity, 131
  in leadership, 137, 138, 165
  and responsibility, 131-133, 136-137
Action
  and accountability, 137
  and choice, 45, 131
  and inspiration, 115
  planning, 244
Adaptation/Adaptability
  in adventure, 1, 6
  to change, 88, 91, 105, 110, 245
  in leadership, 6, 69, 71
  and planning, 19, 105
Adventure
  business and leadership applications of, 5-6, 59
  core elements of, 3, 11
  defining, ix, 1, 3, 11
  integration process, 244
  mindset, *see Mindset, adventure*
  personal stories of, ix, 1, 4, 35-37, 43-44, 93-95, 104-105, 141-142, 151-152, 202-207
  profile/threshold, 7
  and risk, 4, 5, 11, 36, 103, 113, 202
Adversity, 41, 62, 100, 118, 122
Ahupua'a (Hawaiian land division system), 172
AI (Artificial Intelligence), 2, 18, 59-62
Alignment
  with authenticity, 38
  of values, 58, 60
  with vision, 123

Amundsen, Roald, 144-145
Anicca (impermanence), 13
Annapurna, 174, 202
Antarctica, 50, 66-68, 70, 252
Anxiety, 19, 83, 90, 96, 108
Appreciation, 151-158
Arrogance, 200-202, 212
Arthur, W. Brian, 59
Aristotle, 55
Assumptions
   and blind spots, 28-29
   checking, 28, 106, 197-198
   questioning, 87, 106
Ataraxia (tranquil composure), 96
Aurelius, Marcus, 45, 132
Authenticity
   challenges to, 39-40
   cultivating, 41-42
   defining, 35
   dimensions of, 39
   and leadership, 39, 119
   and vulnerability, 38-39, 41
Awareness
   cultivating, 29-34, 90, 92
   layers of (self, situational, emotional, systemic), 25-27
   in nature, 24, 89, 236
   of self, 25-27, 29, 39, 139
   as seeing vs. looking, 23

B

Ballard, Robert, 145

Bancroft, Ann, 173-174
Bell, Gertrude, 163
Bennis, Warren, 119
Berry, Thomas, 239
Blind spots, 28-29
Branson, Richard, 196-197
Breathing, 30-31, 90, 98, 148
Brezsny, Rob, 156
Brown, Brené, 38
Brown, Donald, 56
Buddha/Buddhism
   and acceptance of change, 13, 132
   and compassion, 81
   and dana (generosity), 128, 160
   and equanimity, 95
   and gratitude, 155
   and interconnectedness, 132
   and Noble Eightfold Path, 55, 114
   and presence, 84
Buckminster Fuller, 125-126, 220
Butterfly Effect, 17

C

Carnegie, Dale, 260
Cialdini, Robert, 162
Change
   acceptance of, 11, 19-20, 95
   accelerating pace of, ix, 2, 17-18
   as constant, 2, 11, 18, 182
   navigating, 19

Index

Chaos
  and change, ix, 1, 59
  chaos theory, 59
  and order, 1
  in VUCA environment, 2
Chouinard, Yvon, 5, 108-109
Christ, Jesus, 80, 135, 228
Christianity, 80, 121, 128, 160, 228, 239
Chief Sealth, 15, 170
Choice
  and accountability, 131
  and attitude, 47
  and conscious decision-making, 46, 50-51
  and reframing ("have to" vs. "get to"), 45
  residing in, 43-51
Clarity, 27, 85, 88
Climbing, see Mountaineering
Collins, Jim, 58
Collaboration
  and authenticity, 36
  and communal self-reliance, 65-76
  and empathy, 78
  and respect, 72
Collective consciousness, 219, 220
Comfort zone, 237, 245, 246
Commitment, 39, 41, 62, 65, 119, 127, 133, 189
Communication
  and authenticity, 38
  and collaboration, 70, 72
  mindful, 41, 91
  in teams, 6, 70
Community
  and accountability, 138
  and collaboration, 65-76
  and inspiration, 121
  and responsibility, 131, 133
Compassion
  and empathy, 77-82
  in leadership, 57
  and service, 128
  and self-care, 79
Complexity Theory, 59, 108, 144
Composure, 96, 98-99
Confidence, 19, 39, 199-213
Confident humility
  vs. arrogance, 200-202
  in leadership, 199, 208-212
  nurturing, 209-212
Conflict resolution, 70-71, 73, 79, 99, 138, 148
Connection
  and authenticity, 38, 41
  and compassion, 77-82
  and empathy, 79
  human, 65, 74, 154
  to nature, 56, 91, 237-238
Consciousness
  collective, 219, 220
  and enlightenment, 230-232
  and presence, 84
  and transformation, 225-227, 230-232, 234, 239-240
  unity, 219, 230

Consensus, 36, 56
Conservation, 16, 81, 117, 161
Contemplation, 30, 80, 98, 189, 229
Cooperation, 19, 56, 72, 177, 220
Courage, ix, 5, 7, 39, 41, 53, 57, 132, 166, 191, 212, 228
Covey, Stephen, 156, 260
Creativity
   and authenticity, 41
   and choice, 46
   and innovation, 191-198
   mindful, 191-198
   and "something else," 191, 193, 228
Culture
   and authenticity, 37
   corporate, 40, 54, 165, 171
   perspectives, 61, 183
   and values, 54, 55, 63
Curiosity
   and adventure, x
   and creativity, 184-185, 197
   and leadership, 172, 186-187
   and learning, 181, 184-185
   and wisdom, 181, 184-185

D

da Vinci, Leonardo, 184-185
Davidson, Richard, 86
Decision-making
   and choice, 43-51
   and discernment, 18, 182
   frameworks for, 6, 99
   and leadership, 6, 70, 99
   process, 58
   and values, 53-63, 122
Discernment, 18, 181-184, 187
Discomfort, 21, 47, 235-236
Disappointment, 5, 31
Diversity, 71, 188
Dreamtime (The Dreaming), 14
Drucker, Peter, 122, 186

E

Earle, Sylvia, 117
Earth, 13, 154, 170, 190
Eckhart Tolle, 85, 182
Ecology, 14, 89, 148, 175, 220
Economics, 2, 16-17, 58, 59, 65, 72, 176, 239
Edison, Thomas, 114
Education, 61, 99, 175, 222
Ego, 41, 54, 128, 219, 227, 229, 230, 239
Einstein, Albert, 15-16
Eisenhower, Dwight D., 110
Elkington, John, 176-177
Empathy
   and compassion, 77-82
   in leadership, 78-79
   and neuroscience, 80
   types of (cognitive, emotional, compassionate), 77
Emotional intelligence, 26-27, 70, 147
Emotions, 13, 19, 27, 31, 32, 39,

Index

41, 77, 86, 96, 100, 120, 134, 148, 164, 234, 235
Empowerment, 39, 78, 83, 119, 129
Energy, 15, 84, 95, 105, 135, 149, 195
Engagement, 46, 58, 72, 83, 87, 116, 133, 148, 171
Enlightenment, 128, 227-232
Entrepreneurship, 1, 60, 184
Environment
  and business ethics, 5, 59, 176
  conservation of, 16, 59, 81, 117, 118, 132
  stewardship of, 138, 170-179
Equanimity
  cultivating, 97-101
  defining, 93, 95
  in leadership, 99
  and neuroscience, 96
Ethics, 5, 55, 57, 63, 81, 165
Everest, Mount, 4, 26, 54, 85, 105, 161, 182, 202
Evolution, 30, 39, 41, 184, 217, 221, 226, 229

F

Failure, 12, 42, 63, 72, 99, 100, 118, 126, 164, 189, 198, 202, 210
Family, 17, 33, 47, 48, 133, 179, 187, 218, 220
Farmer, J. Doyne, 60
Fear
  and adventure, 7
  and authenticity, 41
  and courage, 94
  as information, 94
  and leadership, 122
  overcoming, 31, 48, 94, 96, 118
Flexibility, 4, 19, 29, 71, 88, 97, 105, 109, 111
Flow, 13, 19, 87, 143, 144, 146, 153
Focus, ix, 28, 49, 86, 98, 147, 167, 200, 221, 244-245
Follett, Mary Parker, 123
Forgiveness, 133-135
Frankl, Viktor, 45, 47-48, 122
Franklin, Sir John, 183
Freighthopping, 4, 141-142, 151-152
Fromm, Erich, 191
Fuller, Buckminster, 125-126, 220

G

Generosity
  and community, 160
  cultivating, 165
  defining, 159
  and leadership, 163
  and reciprocity, 159-167
  types of, 161
Giving, 128, 159-163, 165-167
Global challenges, 1, 16, 20, 69, 96, 240

Goodall, Jane, 162
Governance, 60, 73, 133, 165, 176, 239
Gratitude
   and abundance mindset, 156
   and appreciation, 151-158
   cultivating, 123, 156-157, 182, 236
   and neuroscience, 155
   and pronoia, 156
   and spirituality, 155
Greed, 164-165
Greenleaf, Robert K., 119, 129
Growth
   and adventure, 3, 11
   and authenticity, 39, 41
   and choice, 47
   and learning, 3, 29, 70, 136, 148, 189, 210
   personal, 3, 19, 27, 41, 131, 136, 138, 148, 158, 235, 237, 239, 240, 241, 244, 247
Guidance, ix, 32, 89, 129, 162, 171-172, 193

H

Habeler, Peter, 26
Habits, 50, 92, 110, 167, 244-245
Hanh, Thich Nhat, 99
Happiness, 44, 49, 77, 118, 120, 128, 155, 197, 226
Harmony, 14, 24, 27, 55, 99, 134, 160, 182
Healing, 79, 128, 133-135, 138-139, 143, 216
Heart, x, 24, 41, 75, 154, 160, 163, 247
Hierarchy of Needs (Maslow's), 217-222, 227, 230, 240
Hill, Carolynn Marie, 85
Himalayas, 6, 94, 104, 141, 160, 206
Hinduism, 81, 114, 128, 135, 155, 219, 229
Ho'oponopono, 133-135, 139
Honnold, Alex, 6, 53
Honesty, 38, 39, 41, 53, 139
Hope, 48, 68, 70, 115, 119, 120-121
Hope Spots, 117
Humility, 199-213, 217
   See also: Confident humility
Humphreys, Alastair, 154
Hypothermia, 104-105

I

Impermanence, 11, 13, 18-20, 97
Indigenous wisdom
   and community, 56, 128
   and interconnectedness, 14-15
   and navigation, 192-193
   and patience, 143
   and stewardship, 170
   and transformation, 229-230
Individualism, 65, 74, 138
Influence, 51, 122, 148, 162

Index

Innovation
    and adventure, 5
    and creativity, 191-198
    and leadership, 3, 5, 78, 99,
        109, 116, 123, 171, 209
    and values, 59, 62
Inspiration
    and creativity, 113-123, 195
    cultivating, 121-123
    and leadership, 119-121
    and vision, 113-123
Integrity, 27, 38, 39, 57, 110,
    131, 133
Intelligence, emotional, 26-27,
    70, 147
Intention, 31, 55, 107, 196, 220,
    226, 228
Interconnectedness
    and acceptance, 11, 14,
        18-20
    and community, 65, 74
    global, 16-17
    and science, 15
    and spirituality, 13, 133
Internal compass, 32
Intuition, 89, 193, 228
Invention, 113, 184
Islam, 81, 160, 229

J

Journaling, 21, 33, 41, 46, 157,
    205
Joy, 32, 79, 99, 119-121, 152,
    155, 185, 226

Judaism, 81, 132
Jung, Carl, 93, 144, 146
Justice, 16, 131-132, 218, 222

K

Kabat-Zinn, Jon, 97
Kagge, Erling, 85
Karnali River, 1, 11, 35-36, 56,
    104, 249
Karma, 29, 135
Kindness, 37, 80, 123, 160
Knowing, 89, 193
    See also: Intuition
Knowledge, 61, 106, 111, 160-
    161, 183, 192, 198, 218

L

Lao Tzu, 143, 200
Leadership
    and accountability, 137, 138,
        165
    adaptive, 6, 60
    and adventure mindset, 5-6,
        59
    and authenticity, 39, 119
    and choice, 50
    and collaboration, 66-72
    and confident humility, 199,
        208-212
    and empathy, 78-79
    and equanimity, 99
    and inspiration, 119-121
    and presence, 90
    servant, 119, 129

and stewardship, 170-172
and values, 54, 57-58
and vision, 119
Learning, 181
   continuous, 181, 188-190, 247
   from experience, 6, 29, 136, 189
   from failure, 100, 209
   and growth, 3, 29, 70, 136, 148, 189, 210
Life, as adventure, x, 4, 96, 152, 190, 248
Listening, 70, 78, 161, 172, 188, 191
Lorenz, Edward, 17
Love, 41, 56, 77, 80, 119, 127, 135, 160, 216, 226, 229, 237
Luck, 111, 142

M

Management, 57-58, 60, 62, 71, 99, 109, 122, 148, 171, 173, 176, 186
Marquis, Sarah, 8
Maslow, Abraham
   Hierarchy of Needs, 217-222, 227, 230, 240
   and self-actualization, 218, 222
   and self-transcendence, 220, 230, 237, 240
   study of Blackfoot Nation, 221-222
Mead, Margaret, 161

Meditation, 13, 24, 30, 80, 86, 91, 97-98, 107, 155, 226, 230, 234
Meir, Jessica, 21
Messner, Reinhold, 26, 96
Mindfulness
   and communication, 41, 91
   cultivating, 30, 97, 234
   and meditation, 86, 97-98
   and presence, 83, 86, 97
Mindset
   adventure, x, 1-10, 11, 18, 29, 153, 182, 190, 243-248
   fixed vs. growth, 201
Motivation, 3, 19, 54, 71, 79, 116, 120, 122, 148, 171, 240
Mountaineering, 4, 12, 26, 53, 54, 59, 62, 93-95, 105, 145, 161, 192, 249
"Mudita" (sympathetic joy), 155

N

Nansen, Fridtjof, 57
Native Americans, 81, 115, 132, 143, 160, 170, 215
Nature, 1, 4, 12, 30, 43, 173-174, 216, 232
   and awareness, 24, 89, 236
   and connection, 56, 91, 237-238
   and generosity, 159
   and healing, 13, 237-238
   and inspiration, 123

Index

and presence, 88-89, 91
stewardship of, 170, 174-175, 238
Navigation
   indigenous techniques, 192-193
   in adventure, 1, 67, 85
Needs, Hierarchy of (Maslow's), 217-222, 227, 230, 240
Nepal, 1, 11, 35, 56, 104, 174, 249
Neuroscience, 46, 80, 86, 96, 147, 155, 164
Non-dual awareness, 90, 230, 232
Nyad, Diana, 12

O

Observation, 15, 33, 41, 95, 181, 192, 235
Optimism, 49, 119
Organizations
   and accountability, 137, 138, 165
   and adventure mindset, 5-6
   culture of, 40, 54, 165, 171
   and leadership, *see* Leadership
   and stewardship, 170-172, 176-177
   and values, 54, 57-58, 62
Ostrom, Elinor, 72-73

P

Patience, Strategic
   balancing with action, 146
   cultivating, 146-149
   defining, 142-143
   and leadership, 148
   and spiritual traditions, 143-144
Peace, 57, 81, 99, 240
Perception, 26, 87, 134, 154, 217, 226
Perseverance, 4, 113, 121, 190
Perspective
   and adventure, 2
   and empathy, 79
   shifting, 34, 49, 97, 129
   and wisdom, 188
Photography, 23, 203, 206
Polynesian Wayfinders, 192-193, 195
Power, 5, 27, 45, 47, 51, 65, 83, 85, 98, 113, 116, 117, 119, 122, 123, 127, 129, 133, 154, 155, 162, 184, 215, 227
Practice, 13, 21, 29, 30-34, 41, 49-50, 55, 81, 86, 90-92, 97-98, 107, 111, 123, 133, 146, 148, 155-157, 166, 188, 209, 229, 234-239, 241, 243, 244-245, 247
Presence
   cultivating, 83-92
   defining, 83
   in leadership, 119
   and nature, 88-89, 91
   and neuroscience, 86
Problem-solving, 3, 6, 11, 41, 68, 71, 186

Pronoia, 156
Purpose
  and inspiration, 113, 121
  and meaningful service,
    125-130
  and vision, 27, 41, 63, 69, 89,
    115, 120, 125, 171, 216,
    236, 247

Q
Qigong, 13, 30, 86, 226, 235
Quantum field, 15, 134-135,
  163, 228
Quechua, 170, 229

R
Reciprocity, 56, 159-167
Reflection, 7, 33, 46, 98, 100,
  119-120, 121, 148, 185, 189,
  209, 210, 244, 246-247
Relationships
  and accountability, 136, 139
  and authenticity, 41
  and collaboration, 69-70
  and empathy, 79
  and gratitude, 157
  and stewardship, 179
Resilience
  and adventure, 1, 3, 5, 11
  and choice, 50
  collective, 68
  cultivating, 19, 21, 41, 79,
    100, 122, 138, 147-148,
    158, 164, 173
  in leadership, 6
Respect, 24, 26, 37, 55-56, 65,
  68, 71-72, 109, 133, 163,
  191, 218
Responsibility
  and accountability, 131-133,
    136-137
  and choice, 44, 131
  corporate, 6, 176
  and freedom, 132
  and kuliana, 133
Risk, 4, 5, 11, 36, 48, 53, 54, 57,
  60, 63, 78, 98, 118, 142, 202,
  206, 209, 210, 253
Rumi, Jalāl al-Dīn, 182, 225, 229
Rutkiewicz, Wanda, 54

S
Safety, 38, 39, 42, 53, 60, 69, 74,
  99, 103, 110, 154, 171, 187,
  206, 209, 218
  psychological, 38, 68, 99,
    148, 187, 209
Savage, Roz, 117-118
Scott, Robert Falcon, 144-145
Self-actualization, 218, 222
Self-awareness, 25-27, 29, 39, 139
Self-care, 79, 173
Self-confidence, 19, 39, 199-213
Self-discovery, 35, 41-42
Self-esteem, 41, 136, 218, 222
Self-reliance, 65-76
Senge, Peter, 86
Service, 125-130, 237

Shackleton, Sir Ernest, 66-71, 74
Silicon Valley Bank (SVB), ix-x, 54
Simon, Herbert, 58
Skills
   adventure, 1, 5, 6
   development of, ix, 110-111, 244
   transferable, 5
Social media, 28, 38, 40, 72, 87
Spontaneity, 37, 103-111
Stability, 2, 62, 66
Stewardship
   caring for what sustains, 169-179
   and community, 172-173
   environmental, 138, 170-179
   in leadership, 170-172, 211
   and self-care, 173
   and triple bottom line, 176-177
Stoicism, 95-96, 111, 132, 144
Stone, W. Clement, 135-136
Strategy, 2, 6, 28, 69, 108, 122, 129, 150
Success
   and adventure mindset, 2, 11, 243
   and authenticity, 41
   and choice, 44
   and collaboration, 66
   and confidence, 199
   and gratitude, 156
   in leadership, 5-6, 54, 119

   and values, 53, 58
Suffering, 13, 48, 49, 77, 81, 128, 228, 229
Sufism, 182, 229, 234
Suzuki, Shunryu, x
Synchronicity, 31, 144, 146
Systems thinking, 14, 19, 144

T

Tabei, Junko, 161, 182-183
Tai Chi, 30, 98, 229, 235
Taoism, 81, 143-144, 182, 229
Teamwork, 6, 66, 68-71, 173
Technology, 1, 2, 5, 17, 18, 20, 59, 62, 69, 86, 109, 117, 145, 176, 181, 199, 240
Tikkun Olam (repairing the world), 132
Toffler, Alvin, 2
Tolle, Eckhart, 85, 182
Tragedy of the commons, 72-73
Transcendence
   and enlightenment, 227-232
   and transformation, 225-241
   and Vision 2.0, 219
Transformation
   and adventure, 12
   and consciousness, 225-227, 230-232, 234, 239-240
   defining, 225-226
   and personal growth, 132, 148, 158
   practices for, 235-240
   spiritual, 228-232

Transparency, 38, 39, 60, 70, 110, 165, 208
Trust, 37, 38, 41, 56, 60, 72, 88, 98, 129, 131, 136, 148, 163, 164, 193, 209, 212, 222

U

Uncertainty
 and adventure, 3, 5, 8, 11
 and change, ix, 1, 3
 and leadership, 6
 and planning, 111
 and presence, 29, 87, 193
Understanding, 14, 15, 27, 55, 61, 71, 77-79, 81, 88, 105, 128, 135, 158, 161, 181, 187, 189, 190, 192, 193, 211, 225, 226, 229, 245, 252

V

Values
 and AI, 59-62
 alignment of, 58, 60
 and culture, 54, 63
 in decision-making, 53-63, 122
 in organizations, 54, 57-58
 universal, 56
Viesturs, Ed, 6, 202
Vision
 1.0 (practical), 113-123, 215, 219
 2.0 (spiritual/transcendent), 113, 215-223
 and inspiration, 113-123
 in leadership, 119
 and purpose, 27, 41, 63, 69, 89, 115, 120, 125, 171, 216, 236, 247
Vision quest, 115, 215-216, 221, 222, 237
Vulnerability, 35, 38-39, 41, 74, 79, 196, 216

W

Watson, Jessica, 154
Way of Nature, 13, 89, 249
Weihenmayer, Erik, 4
Wheatley, Margaret "Meg", 57
Wilcox, Ken, 54-55
Wilderness, 1, 4, 12, 24, 30, 43, 89, 173-174, 216, 232, 238
Wisdom
 ancient, ix, 13, 53, 63, 83, 132, 172, 178, 181-182
 and curiosity, 181, 184-185
 and discernment, 181-184
 indigenous, *see Indigenous wisdom*
 seeking, 181-190
Wonder, 119-121, 151-158, 197, 216
Worsley, Frank, 69
Wu-wei (effortless action), 143-144, 146, 148

Y

Yoga, 86, 98, 226
Yosemite National Park, 6, 53

Z

Zakat (charitable giving), 160
Zen, x, 182
Zero-sum thinking, 66, 71, 74

Mark Stevenson and his company Wisdom Quest LLC, offer consulting services to increase our client's probability of success.

A selection of services includes:

- Business and Innovation Strategy
- Optimizing for Innovation and Organization Agility
- Organizational Culture – It's your market advantage
- Leadership and Stakeholder Alignment
- Lead People, Manage Structure and Systems
- Leadership Advisory, Coaching, Tailored Sessions and Workshops for Individuals and Organizations

Purpose, precision, strategic vision, and principles of an Adventure Mindset will distinguish you and your organization from the typical *business as usual* to being a business that matters, inspires, and leads the way to extraordinary results.

Learn more at www.WisdomQuestLLC.com
Visit this book's website: adventuremindsetbook.com
Connect on LinkedIn: www.linkedin.com/in/marklouisstevenson

Made in the USA
Middletown, DE
20 September 2025